Due to circumstances beyond my control, this book is wilder, funnier, and more outrageous than its predecessor, *Raunchy Riddles*.

All the jokes contained herein are funny. None were excluded for being too dirty, too silly, or too *anything*. If it was funny, in it went. Upon inspection, I am sure you'll agree.

Plow on, enjoy the giggles, and if you love the book . . . tell a friend!

Thanks!
Jackie "922-WINE" Martling

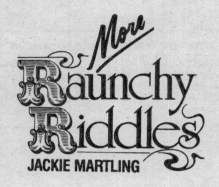

More Raunchy Riddles

JACKIE MARTLING

PINNACLE BOOKS   NEW YORK

MORE RAUNCHY RIDDLES

Copyright © 1985 by Jackie Martling

All rights reserved, including the right to reproduce this book or portions thereof in any form.

An original Pinnacle Books edition, published for the first time anywhere.

First printing/May 1985

ISBN: 0-523-42536-8
Can. ISBN: 0-523-43485-5

Printed in the United States of America

PINNACLE BOOKS, INC.
1430 Broadway
New York, New York 10018

9   8   7   6   5   4   3   2   1

To Dot and John—
for countless reasons,
the main ones being I love them dearly,
and they're both funnier than me.

And thanks to Nancy—
for all her assistance in
writing, editing, and assembling. . . .
By the way, I love her too.

I.

What's pink and moist and split in the middle?
A grapefruit!

How did the pygmy boxer win all his fights?
He'd fill his mouth with ice and cold-cock his opponents!

*

What sign would the madam hang on the brothel door if there was only one girl still available?
"Last butt not leased!"

*

Why wasn't the Polack worried after they gave him a test to see if he was the father of a teenage girl's baby?
Because the doctor took the blood sample from his finger!

*

How does everybody know when you've let loose a really powerful fart in line at the supermarket?
The lady behind you is checking her eggs again!

*

What should a girl do if she has sticky drawers?
Call a carpenter!

*

What's 6.9?
A good thing broken up by a period!

*

Why did the girl compliment her boyfriend on his new moustache?
It made her feel good!

*

What would you call gay sperm?
Fruit juice!

2

How many New Yorkers does it take to change a light bulb?
Go fuck yourself!

*

What's bigamy?
One wife too many. Same as monogamy!

*

What happened to the schoolboy who fooled around with the schoolgirl during the wrong period?
He got caught red-handed!

*

If a dog is happy, he'll wag his tail. What will a goose do?
Make him growl!

*

What's the noisiest thing in the world?
Two skeletons fucking on a tin roof in a hailstorm using soup cans for rubbers!!

*

What did the hostess know when one of the previous night's guests called and asked her if she had a golden toilet?
That *he* was the culprit that had shit in her husband's tuba!

*

Why was the guy who had a nymphomaniac on his waterbed screaming for help?
Because she was going down for the third time!

*

Why do most men like big tits and small pussies?
Because they have big mouths and small dicks!

What would you call a girl who comes on like a sex maniac, but backs out when the chips are down?
A pseudonymph!

*

What's the difference between a quarterback and a virgin bride?
The quarterback *reels* when the *squad* breaks through!

*

What should you do if the secret word is penis?
Don't let it slip out!

*

How do crabs leave the hospital?
On crotches!

*

What tool is about six inches long, has hair on one end, gets stuck in a fleshy crack, and rubbed back and forth before white juicy stuff comes out?
A toothbrush!

*

Why are all hookers apathetic?
They don't give a fuck for nothing!

*

What's a Polish blowjob?
When the girl farts during anal sex!

*

Why is strip poker a great game?
The more you lose, the more you have to show for it!

4

What did the bull say to the nearsighted milkmaid?
"Moooooooooooooooooo!"

*

Why did the exhibitionist get arrested at Burger King?
He drove up to the take-out window and took it out!

*

Why do Arab women wear veils?
So they can blow their noses without getting their hands dirty!

*

How can you tell if a church is gay?
Only half the congregation is kneeling!

*

When a man takes off his pants in a hotel room what's the first
thing to hang out?
The *Do Not Disturb* sign!

*

What's the worst thing about dating a lady leper?
She can only give you head once!

*

What do you spend at a pay toilet?
The going price!

*

What's six inches long, has two nuts, and can make a woman
fat?
An Almond Joy!

*

What's the new Eddie Murphy movie where he plays an undercover cop?
Incognegro!

*

Why did the faggot cross the road?
To get to another fly!

*

What's worse for a girl than having her date disappointed in her?
Having her date in her, disappointed!

*

Why do truck drivers make great lovers?
They know the best places to eat!

*

What's man's greatest invention?
Woman's virtue!

*

What would you call a flashy pianist who fell apart after his last concert?
Leperace!

*

What's fast food in Transylvania?
A tampon pizza!

*

What's every galley slave's nightmare?
A captain that likes to water ski!

Why was the sailor covered with sand?
He was blown under the boardwalk by a Wave!

*

Why are Australian dogs the fastest in the world?
Because the trees are so far apart!

*

Why are cowgirls so wild?
While other girls were having Sex Ed., they were having Mr. Ed!

*

What do they call an Oriental blowjob?
Gobbledegook!

*

What did they sing at Walt Disney's funeral?
"Freeze A Jolly Good Fellow"!

*

What's the difference between a light bulb and a sports car?
It's easy to screw in a light bulb!

*

What does a guy with no arms and no legs do when he gets a hard-on?
Uses it for a kickstand!

*

How does a shithead solve a problem?
He puts on his thinking crap!

*

What makes a party great?
If everybody comes!

*

What's the difference between a soldier searching for his bunk
and a soldier doing what he likes to do best?
A soldier searching for his bunk is on a *cot hunt*!

*

How can you tell if an Alaskan turtle is bombed?
He's trying to fuck an igloo!

*

Why did they put television sets in the Polish ballpark?
So the fans could see what was happening in their local bar!

*

What would you call a proctologist who moonlights as a
fortune teller?
The Fecal Finger of Fate!

*

When do you know a girl is *really* horny?
She sits on your open hand and it feels like a horse is eating out
of your palm!

*

Why should people be more careful with cocaine?
It's nothing to sneeze at!

*

How did Helen Keller go bonkers?
Trying to read a golf ball!

Why did the young girl go to the sperm bank?
For an ice pop!

*

What's the best reply when somebody calls you a mother-fucker?
"Keep your mother out of my yard and I'll keep my yard out of your mother!"

*

Why should a company hire a psychiatrist *and* a proctologist?
To fix their odds and ends!

*

Why do generals put epileptic infantrymen in the front?
So the enemy can't tell who's been shot!

*

Why did the fag pull out his wang in the dentist's chair?
There was a tooth in it!

*

What's the saddest thing about trust going out of a relationship?
It takes all the fun out of lying to each other!

*

Why do Chinese men get a boner when they put their dicks in a light socket?
Erectricity!

*

Where do tobacco-chewing race car drivers refuel?
At spit stops!

What did the nun say to the priest who was teaching her how to swim?
"Father, will I really sink if you take your fingers out?"

*

What's the New York City discotheque for tourists?
The Go-Go Fuck Yourself!

*

What happens when you drink too many Black Russians?
You get hammer-and-sickle cell anemia!

*

What's the easiest way to meet people at a bar?
Pick up somebody else's change!

*

What happened to the Greek gardener?
He got pricked by the rose bushes!

*

What should you do if an elephant's coming?
Stick your finger in his ass!

*

Why do they call athletic shirts *jerseys*?
Because they usually stink!

*

What's the best way to go bald?
Do U-turns under the sheets!

*

What would you call a champion masturbator who's too old to jerk off?
A ex-spurt!

*

What's a premature ejaculation?
A spoilspurt!

*

Where would you see the Jack-off Olympics?
On *The Wide World of Spurts*!

*

What did they call it when Charles Lindbergh had an orgasm while landing in Paris?
The Spurt of St. Louis!

*

What did the Polack say to himself as he looked at The Tomb Of The Unknown Soldier?
"Gee, his family must be proud!"

*

What's a fag's favorite zoo animal?
The chimp-pansies!

*

What's black and white and hairy?
Sister Mary Cunt!

*

What are nymphomaniacs?
People. People who need pee poles!

What did the professor do for the college girl that was having trouble with Sex Ed.?
Kept her after class and pounded it into her head!

*

What's a white mule?
A honky donkey!

*

How is a barbed wire fence like a bikini?
It protects the property, but doesn't obstruct the view!

*

How do Eskimos have children?
They rub noses, and the little buggers fall out!

*

What would you call boobs on a bullfighter?
Matador knobs!

*

What do you get when you goose a ghost?
A handful of sheet!

*

What happened to the girl who had three chances to get pregnant?
Blew 'em all!

*

Where does a horny Indian couple go?
To The Happy Humping Grounds!

*

What would you call a lesbian's I.U.D.?
A fruit loop!

*

When do you know you're *really* a wreck?
When you need two shots of bourbon to calm down enough to get the top off of your valium bottle!

*

Why did the girl come on to the track star?
Because when he told her he had Athlete's Foot, she thought he had said he had *at least* a foot!

*

What's the official bumper sticker of The Polish Rifleman's Association?
"Guns Don't Kill People. Bullets Kill People!"

*

What's a Honeymoon Cocktail?
Seven-Up in cider!

*

When do you know premature ejaculation is a problem?
When you start squirting while she's still flirting!

*

How do you find out who gives the best blowjobs?
Word of mouth!

*

How can you tell if a girl is half-Irish and half-Italian?
She mashes potatoes with her feet!

How would Dirty Johnny use the words *avenue, sister, butter, panther* and *piston* in the same sentence?
"I avenue sister, butter panther already piston!"

*

How many successful jumps do you need to join The Skydiver's Association?
All of them!

*

What do you need to be a disco dancer?
A good rear for music!

*

How is a man's pecker like a door?
When he's not pushing it, he's pulling it!

*

What would you call a guy with no arms and no legs that holds up a bank?
Rob!

*

What's the game show for muffdiving experts?
Name That Tuna!

*

Why did the Jewish American Princess have her teeth filled with gold?
Because she knew her husband would never come into money!

*

How did Gene Barry get the lead role in the terrific gay musical, *La Cage Aux Folles*?
He was obviously in the wrong place at the right time!

14

What do you get when you eat onions and beans?
Tear gas!

*

Do men like women who are deep?
It depends on which end we're talking about!

*

What's The Logger's Credo?
"Tank her, spank her, plank her, shank her, and thank her!"

*

How can you tell if you have incredibly bad breath?
When you talk, people duck!

*

How do you make love toothpaste style?
The guy squirts it out of his tube and onto her brush!

*

What's puberty?
When boys and girls hair their differences!

*

What does a man who's just had an orgasm have in common
with the woman he's on top of?
They both want to get off!

*

What did the dumb wife say when she found out her husband
had a gay lover?
"What's *he* got that *I* haven't got?"

15

What's the main difference between baseball and politics?
In baseball, if you get caught stealing, you're out!

*

Do blacks really talk funny?
No. It be a miff.

*

What do an umbrella and a dick have in common?
They both have to be up to be of service!

*

What would you call a brothel chain that specializes in cunnilingus?
Furburger King!

*

Who works the late shift in the pajama factory?
The nightie watchman!

*

What's an indication that a guy is a real sex maniac?
He won't eat a doughnut unless there's hair on it!

*

Why don't Jewish girls swallow?
They want to be the spitting images of their mothers!

*

What did the Polish girl say when her boyfriend told her that he suffered from premature ejaculation?
"I don't care what you did when you were a kid!"

*

Why didn't the nearsighted woman ever change her son's diapers?
So she could find him!

*

What's a Saturday Night Safari?
Head first into the bush!

*

What's misery for a middle-aged woman?
Borrowing her neighbor's douche bag and finding her husband's false teeth in it!

*

How do they advertise aspirin for masochists?
"Slow, slow relief!"

*

What's worse than leaving your bedpartner unsatisfied?
Leaving your bedpartner, unsatisfied!

*

What happened when a streaker ran up to three nuns who were standing on a street corner?
The first nun had a stroke . . . the second nun had a stroke . . . but the third nun didn't touch him!

*

What would you call a homosexual's lubricant jelly?
A queering aid!

*

What's the best kind of girl to take golfing?
One that knows how to use the woods!

Why do men like girls from Australia?
They're nicer down under!

*

What did Minnie Mouse sing when she caught Mickey with Daisy Duck?
"M-I-C- . . . K-E-Y . . . O-U S-O-B!"

*

What do you call wearing a condom to have anal sex?
Brown bagging it!

*

Who's the girl to meet at Ocean World?
The one that teaches the blowfish!

*

What would you call a chicken that was incubated in an outhouse?
A toilet peeper!

*

If horse racing is the Sport of Kings, what is the Sport of Queens?
Drag racing!

*

What did the epileptic do when he found out he had leprosy?
Went to pieces!

*

Why are swap clubs so popular?
There are no dues and very few don'ts!

What would you call a black guy with no arms and no legs floating in the water?
Buoy!

*

Why are there so few cannibals around anymore?
They've discovered sixty-nine!

*

What is the fear of being jerked off by a tiger?
Clawstrophobia!

*

What's the opposite of progress?
Congress!

*

What's a Roman streetwalker's motto?
"Never let a Dago by!"

*

Why did they come out with designer laxatives?
For people who like to go in style!

*

What was the movie about a girl whose father was sexually attracted to the black guy she brought home to meet the family?
Goose Who's Coming To Dinner!

*

Why did the midget save the filters from his cigarettes?
His fiancée used them for tampons!

*

How did the Jewish American Princess know her parents were anxious for her to get married?
They gave her towels that said, "Hers" and "Watch this space"!

*

What's a miniskirt?
A bum wrap!

*

What does a Polack play on his Walkman?
"Left foot, right foot, left foot, right foot . . .!"

*

What's the proper way to refuse the sperm bank when they come to your door for a contribution?
Tell them you give the united way!

*

How was the symbol for infinity inspired?
By a fat hooker sitting naked on a mirror!

*

What should you do if your wife has triplets?
Go out and find those other two guys!

*

How can you catch a living bra?
Set a booby trap!

*

What's the difference between Joan Collins and the Titanic?
Only about 1000 people went down on the Titanic!

What's grosser than opening the refrigerator door and having a rump roast fart in your face?
Biting into a jelly doughnut and noticing a string dangling out of it!

*

How does a Jewish man know that sex is more play than work?
If it was more work than play, his wife would have a schvartze in to do it!

*

What did the reporter say after he interviewed two hundred virgins?
"Today, life was just a poll of cherries!"

*

Why are there so many Chinese in the world?
If you don't know, you've obviously never tried to do your own shirts!

*

What's the cheapest way to get a tonsillectomy?
Gargle with Preparation H!

*

What's the difference between a mistress and a wife?
The difference is night and day!

*

When do your farts have that pipe organ effect?
After you eat macaroni with beans!

*

What do gay pirates sing?
"Yo, ho, ho and a bottle of cum!"

*

What's an Italian 10?
No moustache!

*

What do you call obscene writing on the wall?
Pornograffiti!

*

What did Dirty Johnny's father answer when Johnny asked him what wife swap meant?
"Go next door and ask your mother!"

*

What's the new bra that offers total freedom of motion to well-endowed ladies?
The Jonathan Livingston C Cup!

*

Why do girls with big noses get a lot of dates?
Easy pickings!

*

Why should you let people masturbate in peace?
They're only screwing themselves!

*

What's an inner city program you definitely would *not* want your teenage daughter joining?
Head Start!

What's black and white and sees eye to eye?
Sammy Davis and Sandy Duncan!

*

What did the gay write on the postcard he sent to his straight roommate while vacationing alone in Europe?
"Wish you were queer!"

*

What's a diaphragm?
A trampoline for schmucks!

*

Why do Italians talk with their hands?
Because their breath could take the curl out of your pubic hair!

*

What disease do gay monsters get?
Ghoul-AIDS!

*

What do you get when you cross a donkey with an onion?
A piece of ass that brings tears to your eyes!

*

What's the height of nerve?
Shitting on someone's doorstep, then ringing and asking for toilet paper!

*

How is a hooker like Johnny Carson?
They both make their money on the tube!

*

What is West Coast screwing?
Californicating!

*

What happened when the girl was marooned on a desert island with three guys?
After a week, she was so ashamed of what she was doing she killed herself.
After two weeks, the guys were so ashamed of what they were doing they buried her.
After three weeks, they were so ashamed of what they were doing they dug her up again!

*

What did the Polack do when he heard there was going to be a show on T.V. about venereal disease?
Tried to catch it!

*

What did the genie say to the ugly girl?
"Ptttooie! Now, what was your second wish?"

*

How can you *really* get some kicks?
Lace up your ass and rent it to the NFL!

*

What's invisible and smells like worms?
Bird farts!

*

How strong is the wind in Chicago?
Well, one day it stopped, and everybody fell down!

*

What do you call it when a fag sticks a Barbie up his ass?
A doll-do!

*

What's a bigamist?
A man who keeps two himself!

*

What did the leper say at the fancy restaurant?
"Could I have another finger bowl? Mine is full!"

*

What would you call an adolescent rabbit?
A pubic hare!

*

What are head waiters?
The guys in line at a gang bang!

*

What's prune juice?
The *run*-cola!!

*

Why did the Polish water polo team have to drop out of the Olympics??
All the horses drowned!!

*

What would you call a girl that puts in her diaphragm crooked?
Mommy!

*

What would you call a guy with no arms?
Why call? He can't answer the phone anyway!

*

What's the hippie ice cream flavor?
Mocha joint!!

*

Who had the first computers?
Adam and Eve! Eve had an apple, and Adam had a wang!

*

If a large bra is a C cup, what's a large jock?
A dick C cup!

*

How did the Jewish American Princess get her Ph.D. in six months?
She married him!

*

What prehistoric comic strip character had diarrhea between buildings?
Alley Ooooooooop!

*

What's the difference between a dry, white, Italian wine and a New Jersey stud?
One's a Soave Bolla and the other is a suave bowler!

What was the first evidence of homosexuality in the Revolutionary War??
Benny dicked Arnold!

*

Why are women amazing?
They give milk without eating hay, they bleed without getting cut, and they bury bones without digging holes!

*

What's a semi-quickie?
Half-fast sex!

*

What would you call a gay that likes to fuck men with hemorrhoids??
A pile driver!

*

What did George Gershwin write after he put the bottle of mucilage on his pecker?
"Rhapsody in Glue!"

*

What should a girl bring if her boyfriend invites her over for a bite?
Her kneepads!

*

What's Pakistani chicken shit?
Hindu hen doo!

*

Why is it so easy to turn on Frankenstein's monster?
Because he has amps in his pants!

*

What's the difference between a circus and a burlesque?
A circus is a cunning bunch of stunts!

*

Why couldn't the leper take a dump after the comedy show?
Because he'd laughed his ass off!

*

What do you call it when you have sex with the person that brings you your car?
Valet porking!

*

What happened to the horny tax accountant?
He wrote himself off!

*

What do you get when you cross an underwear factory with *The Love Boat*?
A panty-liner!

*

What did the guy say when his date wouldn't blow him or fuck him?
"Taste not, want not!"

*

Why did the homosexual taking a dump in the woods think he had just had a miscarriage??
When he looked down, he had done his diarrhea on a frog!

Which two of the following won *Best Rhymes of the Times* in *1954*?

He loves me . . . he don't! He'll have me . . . he won't!
He would if he could but he can't . . . so he don't!

*

A delightful sunbather from Kester,
Clad just as nature had dressed her,
Strolled boldly through town,
To get her skin brown.
Cops fought for their turn to arrest her!

*

Oh sole mio,
I've got VD, oh.
And when I pee, oh!
Oh! Mama Mio!

*

The sexual urge of the camel is greater than anyone thinks.
And often, in times of passion,
   he'll attempt to bugger the Sphinx.
But the Sphinx's posterior entrance
Is blocked by the sands of the Nile,
Which accounts for the lump on the camel
And the Sphinx's inscrutable smile!

*

What is the best indication that a man is incredibly hung?

1. He works as a speed bump.
2. He goes to his company picnic and wins the three-legged race . . . solo.
3. When he walks out of the shower it looks like he's playing cricket.
4. He steals second base without leaving first.
5. He keeps his tool on a spool.
6. He has a job wrecking buildings with his dick.

Match The Cocktails

Play bartender!
Match the names with the results of your concockting!

_____ 1. The Rumrunner
_____ 2. The Patrick Henry
_____ 3. A Shakespeare
_____ 4. Virgin's Downfall
_____ 5. Hobo Highball
_____ 6. Screw Mrs. Olson
_____ 7. The New Yorker
_____ 8. Sunburn Swizzle
_____ 9. Poker Cocktail
_____10. Orient Express
_____11. An Outfielder
_____12. Avis Eggnog
_____13. The Money Belt
_____14. The Trash Collector Collins
_____15. Hurry, Mary!
_____16. Judge Julep
_____17. The Falsie Jubilee
_____18. A Flaming Michael Jackson
_____19. The Three Stooges

a. Saki and prune juice
b. Two sips and you act like a boob
c. A few slugs, and *she'll* pay *you*
d. Make her #2, then try a little ardor
e. After just two sips, she's the "ho", and you're the "bo"
f. A Pepsi and a piece of fruit . . . and you'll be lit
g. Three sips and she'll raise you to see how badly you want to be in
h. Coffee and orange juice
i. After the belt she goes for your fly
j. Cherry wine with a banana in it
k. Three sips and she'll put something out
l. She lets you pay for it, and then tells you to go fuck yourself
m. Vodka and prune juice
n. One sip and she gives you liberties (a revolutionary drink)
o. A glug and she makes a play for you
p. She smells it and instantly goes down on you
q. Bacardi and prune juice
r. Two shots and your honor
s. After three she starts peeling
t. Jack Daniels, George Dickel, and Ronald Reagan

Polish jokes are fun, but there are always some people who think they've heard them all. So, a little challenge is in order. If you've heard them, there's no need to go searching for the answers. If you haven't, find the correct response across the page!

_____ 1. What would you call a modern Polish airliner?
_____ 2. Why did the Polish lady put her head in the freezer?
_____ 3. Why did the Polack only water half his lawn?
_____ 4. How do you know if a burglar is Polish?
_____ 5. Why did the Polack keep empty beer cans in his refrigerator?
_____ 6. Why did the Polack cross the road?
_____ 7. What do you get if you cross a Polack and a flower?
_____ 8. Why did the Polack buy his wife steel wool?
_____ 9. What was the Polish skydiver's misfortune?
_____10. How can you tell the Polack at the batting range?
_____11. Why did the Polack buy an electric lawn mower?
_____12. Why did the Polack cut a hole in his umbrella?
_____13. What does a Polack call his pet zebra?
_____14. How do you confuse a Polish laborer?
_____15. What's the first thing a Polack does after a shower?
_____16. Why don't Polacks throw dinner parties?
_____17. How can you tell if a firing squad is Polish?
_____18. How can you tell if a beekeeper is Polish?
_____19. Why are games like this such a pain in the ass?

*

Answers:

_____a. They can't spell RSVP!
_____b. He knocks!
_____c. So he could find his way back to the house!
_____d. Spot!
_____e. He wanted her to knit him a stove!
_____f. To frost her hair!
_____g. I don't know!
_____h. Gets out of those wet clothes!
_____i. His honey has hives!
_____j. His snorkle didn't open!
_____k. Lay out three shovels and tell him to take his pick!
_____l. He heard there was a 50% chance of rain!
_____m. They stand in a circle!
_____n. To get to the middle!
_____o. So he could see if it stopped raining!
_____p. A Dumbo jet!
_____q. For his friends that didn't drink!
_____r. A blooming idiot!
_____s. He's the one looking for first base!
_____t. So he could see if there was a 50% chance of fucking Spot!

The Most Romantic Hit Song of 1959 was . . .

_____ 1. *You Were Never Lovelier, And I Think It Stinks*

_____ 2. *I Proposed To Her In The Garage, And She Couldn't Back Out*

_____ 3. *She Spilled Her Tom Collins And Lost Her Cherry Under The Table*

_____ 4. *I Took Her Out Into The Fog And Mist*

_____ 5. *I Can't Leave Her Behind Alone*

_____ 6. *I Used To Kiss Her On The Lips, But It's All Over Now*

_____ 7. *She Was Only The Florist's Daughter, But She'd Let Anyone Sniff Her Bloomers*

_____ 8. *Wowie Keeflowie, Am I Fucking Horny*

_____ 9. *I'm In The Mood To Get Nude, It May Be Lewd, Rude And Crude, But I'm Stewed And I Want To Get Suntan*

*

What is *foreplay*?

_____ 1. The loving before the shoving

_____ 2. The petting before the getting

_____ 3. Bullshit

_____ 4. The licking before the pricking

_____ 5. The stroking before the poking

_____ 6. The procrastination and masturbation preceding penetration

_____ 7. The lingering and the fingering

_____ 8. Making out before you fuck

_____ 9. A premature ejaculator's nightmare

_____10. Unnecessary with barn animals

*

Which of the following was *The Most Off the Wall Graffiti of 1982*?

_____ 1. "I'm a vampire, please wash your neck!"

_____ 2. "If Ella Fitzgerald married Darth Vader, she'd be Ella Vader!"

_____ 3. "Whistler's mother was framed!"
_____ 4. "Bad spellers of the world untie!"
_____ 5. "Marie Antoinette gave head!"
_____ 6. "I'm black with eleven inches!"
       Underneath: "I'm green with envy!"
_____ 7. "Nathan Hale was hung!"
_____ 8. "A woman's place is on my face!"
_____ 9. "I want this to be in a book!"

*

Which of the following is the best expression for an Oriental male homosexual?

_____ 1. Gob Ling
_____ 2. Wang Lung
_____ 3. Dickie Chin
_____ 4. Dong Chu
_____ 5. Ah So Ling
_____ 6. Goo Tung
_____ 7. Wun Hung Gai
_____ 8. Wang Chu
_____ 9. Dickie Tung
_____10. Goo Chin
_____11. Gob Chu
_____12. Et Cetera
_____13. Bruce

*

Which three of the following would be enough to nominate a learning institution for The Breeder's Digest Wildest School In North America Sweepstakes?

_____ 1. The year's first composition is _Who I Did Over Summer Vacation._
_____ 2. Every morning they have Blow and Tell.
_____ 3. Every morning they have Show and Smell.
_____ 4. There's graffiti on the teachers' skirts.
_____ 5. The school paper has an obituary column.
_____ 6. They teach Driver's Ed. and Sex Ed. in the same car.

_____ 7. They catch you playing with yourself, send you to the Principal's office and he finishes you off.

_____ 8. Every afternoon they have Farts and Drafts.

_____ 9. The only reason they have recess is to carry out the wounded.

_____10. The best mark you can get is fuckin' A.

*

Of the following, which is the *best* evidence that a girl has gotten *really* fat?

_____ 1. Her eyelids squeak.

_____ 2. She drives over a bump, and there's no bump.

_____ 3. She jumps in your Jacuzzi and blocks all the jets.

_____ 4. She looks like she swallowed a house with all the doors open.

_____ 5. You take her skiing and have to buy her a forklift ticket.

_____ 6. She walks onto the beach in a bikini and Sumo wrestlers snicker.

_____ 7. Rodney Dangerfield looks at her and bellows, "What a crowd!"

_____ 8. When she walks around New York City, helicopters report where she is.

_____ 9. You take her to a ball game and the vendors draw straws to see who gets your section.

_____10. Her front door has stretch marks.

_____11. When she walks, people listen.

_____12. She clips her toenails with an electric can opener.

_____13. She goes to a fat farm and comes home with a blue ribbon.

_____14. Her LaCoste shirt sports a brontosaurus.

_____15. While jogging, she gets a ticket for passing a school bus.

_____16. Her idea of a diet is grazing with her teeth out.

_____17. She wears a bell around her neck.

_____18. She has double shins.

_____19. She eats much more than everybody else.

*

Which of the following is the proper way to send a fag off on an ocean cruise?

_____ 1. "Buns voyage!"
_____ 2. "Bone voyage!"
_____ 3. "Good gobs of naval gravy!"
_____ 4. "Cankers aweigh!"
_____ 5. Jerk off in his mouthwash
_____ 6. "Hope you find someone to stick their cock in your asshole!"
_____ 7. "Go fuck yourself!"
_____ 8. "Don't forget to ride!"
_____ 9. "Here's mud on your helmet!"

*

Which of the following questions is *The Most Obvious "Yes" Answer Of The Baby Boom Generation*?

_____ 1. Does a barbeque nut love the grate outdoors?
_____ 2. Does Bobby Fischer have a checkered past?
_____ 3. Did Snow White have 7-Up every night?
_____ 4. Does a sperm bank donor pull a boner?
_____ 5. Is the gynecology business looking up?
_____ 6. Does a Greek neighbor come in the back door?
_____ 7. Is a premature ejaculator a troubled shooter?

*

What is the all-time, most-used expression for the penis?

_____ 1. Pink eel
_____ 2. Trouser snake
_____ 3. Dick
_____ 4. One-eyed wonder worm
_____ 5. Shadroul
_____ 6. Crotch squirrel
_____ 7. Schlong
_____ 8. Tallywhacker
_____ 9. Stopper
_____10. Peepee
_____11. Willie
_____12. Love muscle

_____13. Clamdigger
_____14. Dork
_____15. Gherkin
_____16. Schwantz
_____17. Cock
_____18. Cunt hook
_____19. This

*

Which of the following is *not* the actual punch line to a classic joke?

_____ 1. "Good! Perfect shot! Now, take the club out of your mouth, put it in your hands, and we'll go for distance!"
_____ 2. "What? And quit show business?"
_____ 3. "Just fine, doc, except every time I ask her a question, she lifts her leg and says, 'Huh?'"
_____ 4. "That's where they held the auction!"
_____ 5. "The *ARISTOCRATS*!"
_____ 6. "And if it wasn't for the grace of God and these two fingers, I'd have never gotten them back in!"

*

Which of the following is the greatest opening line to a song in The Famous Fifties?

_____ 1. "Love me tender, love me rare.
   Love me in my underwear . . ."

_____ 2. "Hello, young lovers, you're under arrest . . ."

_____ 3. "Open your legs, dear, you're breaking my glasses . . ."

_____ 4. "Davy, Davy got it, and gave it to the whole frontier . . ."

_____ 5. "Mister Sandman, give me a roll
   Of toilet paper, to wipe my asshole.
   I'm sitting here, in gaseous vapor.
   Some son of a bitch stole the toilet paper . . ."

_____ 6. "Ain't it great, after eatin' your date,
   Brushin' your teeth with a comb . . ."

38

II.

What happened to the skinny guy who
went to Alaska?
He came home a husky fucker!

Why did the girl bathe in her hair coloring rinse?
So she'd have a snatch to match!

*

What would you call the masseuse at a reducing salon?
A blubber rubber!

*

What do they call coin-operated robot hookers in Las Vegas?
Slut-machines.

*

Why is the bell a wedding symbol?
Because it has a long dong in it!

*

Why did the waitress gasp when one of her customers told her
she had a tampon behind her ear?
She realized where her pen was!

*

Why did the perverted trumpeter go to the track?
To play the horses!

*

What's the difference between a young hooker and an old
hooker?
Vaseline and Polygrip!

*

When do a lot of men think of their ex-wives?
When they help themselves to a cold buffet!

What do fags call hemorrhoids?
Speed bumps!

*

Why did the groom find his virgin bride crying and pointing to his pecker when he woke up the morning after?
She thought they had used it all up in one night!

*

When is the shit *really* gonna hit the fan?
In the Turd World War!

*

When do you know you have a masturbation problem?
When your psychiatrist calls you Thumper!

*

What would you call an early sixties black singing group that now tours as evangelists?
The Holy Roller Coasters!

*

How do we know that necrophiliacs are lousy lovers?
Their partners never come too!

*

What did The Godfather do when he caught a guy in bed with his wife?
Pulled out a gun and made him a get off 'er he couldn't refuse!

*

Why is dating a divorcee a lot like working on your old car?
You have fun fooling around with used parts!

What did the Jewish man say when his daughter ran up to him and said she needed fifty dollars?
"Forty dollars? What do you need thirty dollars for?"

*

What does it mean when they say a couple slept like spoons?
They flopped around in dirty drawers!

*

What would you call an Indian that sells cocaine?
Chief Running Nose!

*

What's a flat-chested stenographer?
A topographical error!

*

What's the major fringe benefit of being a prostitute?
You never know who you're gonna meat!

*

How does a horny, ugly man describe his sex life?
Fist or famine!

*

Why did the bargain hunter marry the amputee?
Because he was 25% off!

*

What's the easiest way to mount a butterfly?
Get her drunk first!

*

What happened to the guy with no arms that tried to masturbate?
He was stumped!

*

What did the little black kid say as he walked past the zebra?
"Now you see me, now you don't, now you see me . . ."

*

What's making love hot dog style?
A wienie between the buns!

*

Who's *Sesame Street*'s horniest character?
The Nookie Monster!

*

What does it say on St. Peter's answering machine?
St. Elsewhere!

*

What is the suburban version of the Seventh Commandment?
"Thou Shalt Not Omit Adultery!"

*

What do you call it when there's cocaine in the laundry soap?
High Tide!

*

What does a snowgirl get when she blows a snowman?
Ice Cream!

*

What do you have if your mule eats the legs off my rooster?
Two feet of my cock in your ass!

*

What's a highball?
A drink you serve to get somebody high enough to ball you!

*

Who was Alexandria Graham Bellski?
The first long distance callgirl!

*

What did the 96-year-old man say when his doctor told him
that marrying his 21-year-old financée could prove fatal?
"If she dies, she dies!"

*

How does a leper end a poker game?
Throws in his hand!

*

How does a girl get her kicks from a midget?
In the knees!

*

Why did the widow give the traveling salesman a free meal?
He pumped her well!

*

What would you call an airline steward with girlfriends in New
York City and Washington, D.C.?
A shuttlecock!

*

What happened to the Polack who went to the driving range to hit out a bucket of balls?
He broke his driver on the bucket!

*

What's K.Y. jelly??
A hang glider!!

*

Who competed with Archie for Veronica's attention and was a real pain in the ass?
Wedgie!

*

How do you get a date with a mermaid?
Drop her a line!

*

What did they call the congressional page scandal?
Tailgate!

*

What are the two things the urologist could tell you about your girlfriend's specimen?
"Herpes, all right," or "Her pee's all right!"

*

What's the most fun at a picnic?
Getting the nod to put your prod in the pod of a nice bod on the warm sod!

*

What is plasticophobia?
The fear of choking to death on a falsie!

What's more obvious than a hard-on in a bathing suit?
A Kotex on a nudist!

*

What's the worst thing about screwing on a waterbed?
Your plug keeps coming out!

*

What did they call the episode where The Incredible Hulk got punched in the balls?
Green Achers!

*

What's a nice term for a person with herpes?
An incurable romantic!

*

Why does the battle of the sexes wage on and on?
Because husbands usually only get it half the times they want it, and wives usually only want it half the times they get it!

*

What do you call it when a rooster kicks an egg across the barnyard?
Cock soccer!

*

What would you call a woman who no longer finds fault with her husband?
A widow!

*

What do you get when you cross an elephant with a Jewish American Princess?
The world's most expensive nose job!

*

What would you call a woman who cooks carrots and peas in the same pot?
Unsanitary!

*

What would you call a low-class motel?
A humpty dump!

*

What's better than going for a drive to fool around?
Parking somewhere and getting down to business!

*

What would you call a stiff wienie up your fanny?
A cheekbone!

*

How is a promiscuous girl like a doorknob?
Everybody gets a turn!

*

What does the sign say on the door of the artificial insemination clinic?
"Please come in and be seeded!"

*

When do you know you're getting old?
When what you used to do all night long now takes you all night long to do!

*

When do you know you're getting even older?
When what you used to do all night long you now long to do!

*

What would you call two girls in knit halter tops?
A string quartit!

*

Why did the pregnant Polish lady hire a private detective?
To find out if the baby was really hers!

*

What did the commuter do when the gang of gay midgets got on the crowded train?
He just sat there and felt a little queer!

*

What did the small town headlines read when the girl ran away from home in her father's trousers?
"Flees In Papa's Pants!"

*

When do you know you're *really* busy?
You have to pee in the sink while you brush your teeth . . . and you're a woman!

*

What do you call it when you get a fat girl on your waterbed and have a whale of a time?
Harpoontang!

What's an indication that a girl could improve her personal hygiene?
She blows you a kiss and you get a canker sore!

*

What happens if you go to bed with a space frog?
You wake up with star warts!

*

Who's the laziest person in the world?
The farmhand who stands on a stump, screwing a mule, not moving an inch, just hollering, "Giddap! Whoa! Back! Giddap! Whoa! Back!"

*

What's the distinguishing characteristic of the cabbage snatch doll?
You lift its dress and it smells like sauerkraut!

*

What had five rings but never got laid?
The 1984 Limpdicks!

*

What did the husband want to know when his wife marched in and announced that the doctor said she couldn't make love?
How the doctor found out!

*

How does a Greenwich Village fiddler make a living?
He works in restaurants, going from table to table giving bow jobs!

*

What's an asset?
A little donkey!

*

What would you call a young rabbi?
A whopper snipper!

*

Who whistles while he works?
A two-headed faggot!

*

What would you call it if you looked up a girl's skirt and got a
funny feeling that you'd looked up there before?
A deja view!

*

What did the nearsighted man sing at the urinal?
"Oh, How I Miss You Tonight!"

*

What do Richard Pryor, Michael Jackson, and Hot Lips
Houlihan all have in common?
They've all had major burns on their faces!

*

What happens if you swim too long??
You get water in your ear! (Say it again.)

*

What did the leper say to the prostitute?
"Keep the tip!"

*

What did the Polack say when the girl told him that she had an itchy pussy?
"I don't know anything about those little Japanese cars!"

*

Who's more nervous than a nun in a cucumber patch?
A racehorse with a Greek jockey!

*

Is it a sin to have sex before communion?
Only if you block the aisle!

*

How is a pecker like a woman's panties?
A couple of good yanks will get them off!

*

How does a union fairy tale begin?
"Once upon a time and a half . . ."

*

What's the wildest thing about having a date with an epileptic girl?
She might swallow your tongue, too!

*

What's the difference between a woman and a volcano?
A volcano never fakes eruptions!

*

How did the Italian mother react to the news that her new daughter was born with a moustache?
She was tickled!

What T.V. comedian wears his skivvies too tight?
Dickie Smothers!

*

Why isn't Ralph Nader interested in comedy?
He can't recall jokes!

*

Why do bumblebees wear mazzuzas?
So they won't be mistaken for WASP's!

*

What's the difference between a CB'er and a flasher?
A CB'er *tells* you his handle!

*

Why did the gay become a male prostitute?
Because he decided it was time he took it in his head to make
some money!

*

What does a man have in his pants that a woman doesn't want
in her face?
Wrinkles!

*

Why do Polacks bury their dead face down and shallow?
So when the relatives come to picnic at the grave, there's a
place to put the napkins!

*

What's the greatest joy of motherhood?
Getting that way!

Why was the gay guy depressed?
He was so ugly he had to date girls!

*

Do most men prefer panty hose or bare legs?
Something in between!

*

What would you call a satisfied, nearly extinct sea mammal?
A fuck-filled platypus!

*

When do masochists laugh?
When something strikes them funny!

*

Why did Johnny believe his mother's story about having a black sponge between her legs?
Because he saw the lady next door using *hers* to wash his father's face!

*

How is VD like supper on the farm?
You come and get it!

*

What did the octopus say to the octopussy?
"It takes two to tangle!"

*

What do you get when you freeze holy water with a stick in it?
Pope sickles!

*

How long are anecdotes about well-hung congressmen?
Usually they fill a page!

*

What do you get when you cross a lady marijuana dealer with a motel owner?
A little grass shack-up!

*

Why can love be so intoxicating?
It's often made in the still of the night!

*

What's the best can opener?
Ex-lax!

*

What's eight inches long, round, hard, and has a hole in the middle?
A stack of 69 bus tokens!

*

What would you call a guy that farts in the tub and counts the bubbles?
A puff adder!

*

What's a real dilemma??
Being shipwrecked on a deserted island with a porcupine in heat!

*

What do they take in California to calm their nerves during tremors?
Quake ludes!

*

What magazine features stories about incestual masturbation?
Family Circle Jerk!

*

Who's meaner than the guy who put a tack on the electric chair??
The guy that gave Ray Charles a ticket to see Marcel Marceau!

*

What's the bisexual best seller?
Cunts Is Not Enough!

*

What's a nymphomaniac?
A fuckaholic!

*

What's the hardest thing about studying behavior patterns?
Finding someone who behaves!

*

What do they call lover's lane in New Jersey?
A balling alley!

*

Why was the bluefish blue?
The blowfish wouldn't blow!

*

The answer is *measuring cups*. What's the question?
"What was the guy at the beauty contest doing with the ruler?"

*

What's the worst job at the movie theatre?
Sucking the farts out of the seats!

*

What would you call a dyke bar by the train station?
The Stop, Look and Lesbian!

*

Why do hunters make the best lovers?
Because they go deep into the bush, shoot more than once, and eat anything they get!

*

What would you call a smelly gay accountant if you didn't like him?
An S.O.B. C.P.A. with B.O. who gives B.J.'s!

*

Why does a mother get itchy when she passes a maternity clinic?
She remembers when she had a close shave there!

*

What's the French soap opera where all the action takes place in the girls' lavatory?
BIDETS OF OUR LIVES!

*

What did the cat say after she ate the canary?
"That should put a feather in my crap!"

What would you call a kosher swinger's club?
Stop and Smell the Rosens!

*

What's the definition of a *real* loser?
A guy who has a wet dream and catches VD!

*

What would you call a place where prophylactics were prohibited?
Rubber banned!

*

What's the difference between when a girl ties you up and tickles you with a feather and when a girl uses an onion for a dildo?
When a girl ties you up and tickles you with a feather, it's a *kinky stunt*!

*

What's the barber's fraternity?
Hair Pi!

*

What do you get when you feed beans to an ape?
A boomerangutang!

*

What do you call money for the pay toilet?
Johnny cash!

*

What would you call a hooker with a 500-pound John?
Pressed for cash!

What would you call a sadist's prostitute?
Strapped for cash!

*

What would you call it when a hooker fucks a guy with no arms and no legs?
Cash and carry!

*

What would you call a guy who sleeps with every hooker he meets?
A Cashanova!

*

What would you call a horny Eskimo dwarf?
A frigid midget with a rigid digit!

*

What did the Polack say when the doctor told him his wife had given birth to a beautiful baby boy?
"I knew all along she had it in her!"

*

How can you tell that a lesbian bar is really tough?
The pool tables don't even have balls!

*

How are the bathrooms marked at a Dog Show?
Pointers and *Setters*!

*

What kind of man does a sorority girl like?
A guy who likes to go places and undo things!

Why will Calvin Klein's kids follow in his footsteps?
They have designer genes!

*

What did the wife say when her husband kept climbing on her back?
"Stop hounding me!"

*

Why was the two-by-four looking for a knothole?
It was a stud!

*

Why did the girl go to the nude beach?
To snatch a few rays!

*

What would you call a transvestite lion?
Kink of the Jungle!

*

How is heckling at a comedy show a lot like farting in a museum?
It's fun for the guilty party, but it kind of wrecks it for everybody else!

*

How can you tell if a man grew up with sisters?
One of his eyes is shaped like a keyhole!

*

What did the losing high school football team do after the coach told them to pull themselves together?
Marched into the shower and had a circle jerk!

Why doesn't Dolly Parton's husband want any kids?
He already has his hands full!

*

What's a VD specialist?
A misfortune teller!

*

What would you call Chinese gay sex?
Two man chu!

*

Why do fathers advise their sons to always aim high?
So they won't splash on their shoes!

*

What's Uncle Ben's instant aphrodisiac?
Minute Rise!

*

What would you call a horny forest ranger?
A timber wolf!

*

Why did the cop wound the lady right between the thighs?
He was a crack shot!

*

Why was the female honor student upset?
She missed a period!

*

How can you tell if a witch is horny?
Her broomstick takes 16 "d" size batteries!

*

What's the difference between a Parisian ditch digger and a guy who's down on his date?
A Parisian ditch digger is a *French trencher*!

*

What would you call a Chinese philosopher with poison ivy?
It Ching!

*

What do you get when you cross a cat with a turtle?
A snappin' pussy!

*

What's a Hawaiian aphrodisiac?
Sune Tu Laya!

*

What's a toilet for queers?
A fruit bowl!

*

What should you do in case of fallout?
Reinsert and shorten stroke!

*

What's the best way to save a marriage?
Go out and price a few divorce lawyers!

*

What's the most common bird in suburbia?
The extramarital lark!

*

What would you call an Italian after his vasectomy?
A postop Wop!

*

What's a gay policeman's favorite place?
Headquarters!

*

What's another name for a firing squad?
A gang bang bang!

*

Why did the projector blush?
It saw the filmstrip!

*

How is being married like being constipated?
"To have and to hold!"

*

What's the dirtiest item in the bedroom?
The dresser. (It never changes its drawers!)

*

What's the most useless thing on Grandma?
Grandpa!

*

Who won first prize at the literary costume ball?
The couple that went bottomless as *The Pit and the Pendulum!*

*

When they say the best birth control is an apple, do they mean before or after?
Instead!

*

What happens when you take Ex-lax and Spanish fly?
You get hot to trot!

*

How does an adult fairy tale begin?
"Once upon a girl there was a time . . ."

*

What do you call it when a fag sticks a TV dinner up his ass?
An enemeal!

*

What's the difference between a screw and a staple?
I don't know either! I've never been stapled!

*

What would you call a Fire Island cocaine dealer?
The toot fairy!

*

What would you call a bunch of female softball teams?
Bush league!

*

What's a virgin monkey?
A monkey that won't let another monkey monkey around with her monkey!

*

What's the difference between an oral thermometer and a rectal thermometer?
The taste!

*

Why doesn't Pia Zadora work on Halloween?
They can't get a candle in her head!

*

What's the best way for a man to sneak into the house late?
Stomp in, slam the door, storm upstairs, throw open the door, and bellow, "OK, baby, let's fuck!" (She'll pretend to be asleep!)

*

What have the Polacks decided to do about the population explosion?
Sterilize all the storks!

*

How was Picasso originally inspired?
By Helen Keller's first paint-by-the-numbers!

*

What's the 4V Club?
Vip it in, vip it out, vipe it off, and vamoose!

*

What's the 4F Club?
Find 'em, feel 'em, fuck 'em, and forget 'em!

*

How can you tell if a girl has a corkscrew pussy?
Heads turn!

*

What's the first thing you should ask when a nurse walks into your hospital room?
"Friend or enema?"

*

What do fags call condoms?
Seal a meal!

*

A stork brings average size babies. What brought Orson Wells?
A crane!

*

How did Prince Valiant moonlight?
Selling iron chastity belts at fifty dollars a crack!

*

What did the Chinese girl say after she got her marriage license?
"It won't be wrong now!"

*

What's better than a coat check girl with nice hangers?
A cashier with open drawers!

*

Who are the only people that don't tell dirty jokes?
The ones that can't remember them!

What is a woman's definition of making love?
The election to take the injection of a projection with affection
to the mid-section without objection to the connection!

*

How would an Indian describe a large pile of cow flop?
"Heap big!"

*

What's long and black and smells like pussy?
The handle of Billy Jean King's tennis racket!

*

What did the New Yorker say when he returned from Los
Angeles with VD?
"It wasn't worth the drip!"

*

Why didn't the dog want to be de-wormed?
He was afraid the robins would stop giving him rim jobs!

*

What folk group plays at blood drives?
The New Christy Menstruals!

*

What happened to the boy who drank eight cokes?
He burped 7-Up!

*

What happened to the world's horniest man after his wife made
him put on a metal jockstrap?
He went into a topless bar and was killed by shrapnel!

What's the first thing Adam did after he came upon Eve?
Wiped her off with his fig leaf!

*

What's the difference between a plack and a plick?
A plack hangs on a wall, a plick hangs on a Chinaman!

*

What's the difference between pussy and parsley?
You don't eat parsley!

*

What kind of bees give milk?
Boobies!

*

What's the height of precaution?
An old maid putting a condom on a candle!

*

What's a bikini bottom?
A gash mask!

*

When you're driving along the south shore of beautiful Long
Island, how do you know when you've reached Fire Island?
The street lights are pastel!

*

What would you call a stewardess that can have sex in the
bathroom of an airplane?
A flexible flyer!

*

What's the difference between a straight rodeo and a gay rodeo?
At the straight rodeo they yell, "*Ride* them *suckers!*"

*

What would you call a guy that's half-Japanese and half-Polish?
Sumdumfuk!

*

Why do farmers make delicate, yet firm, lovers?
They know how to milk a cow without waking her up!
(Of course, that's against the law in some states!)

*

What would you call a well-hung member of the G.O.P.?
A banana Republican!

*

What's the difference between a porch swing and a pretty girl?
The porch swing *stops* making noise when you pour on the oil!

*

Why were Helen Keller's hands all purple?
She heard it through the grapevine!

*

Are people who commit incest happy?
Relatively!

*

What should a girl do if she doesn't like the wind messing up her hair?
Shave her ass!

What do lesbians study in college?
Cliterature!

*

What did the termite say when he walked into the bar?
"Is the bar tender here?"

*

Why don't Jewish husbands eat pussy?
Beggers can't be chewers!

*

What would you call a guy with no arms or legs floating close to shore?
Doc!

*

What happened to the guy that died at the height of making love?
He literally came to a stop!

*

What do you get when you cross a Marlboro with sperm?
A butt fuck!

*

The answer is thongs. What's the question?
What doeth Frank Thinatra thing?

*

When do you know a girl is overdue to douche?
Her Odor Eaters crawl up her leg!

*

Which of the proceeding prose was unequivocally named
The Craphouse Quote of 1971?

_____ 1. "I'm insecure now, but how long can it last?"
_____ 2. "Telepathy leaves me speechless!"
_____ 3. "Many men smoke, but Foo Man Chu!"
_____ 4. "I'd give my right arm to be ambidextrous!"
_____ 5. "Drugs are the answer! What was the question?"
_____ 6. "I'm a foot long and four inches around!"
         Underneath: "That's wild! How big is your dick?"
_____ 7. "Time flies like an arrow.
         Fruit flies like a banana."

*

Which of the following is a borderline creative response
to the unbelievably juvenile yet never tiresome greeting,
"How's it hangin'?"

_____ 1. "Low and loose, full of juice, ready for a hairy
         moose . . ."
_____ 2. "Hornier than Santa's reindeer, with a bigger bag of
         goodies . . ."
_____ 3. "Long as a mop, hard as a hatchet, so damned hard
         the cat can't scratch it . . ."
_____ 4. "Under my shirt, far from inert, ready to insert and
         squirt . . ."
_____ 5. "Out of my fly, hard and high, ready to pry or shoot
         in your eye . . ."
_____ 6. "Long and sleazy, ready to go in easy and come out
         greasy . . ."
_____ 7. "Long and fine, like Tarzan's vine, ready for a Jane
         to dine . . ."
_____ 8. "Go fuck yourself . . ."

*

Which of the following descriptions correctly answers the classic question, "How are women like the continents of the earth?"

_____ 1. From 13-18, they're like Africa:
Virgin, unexplored territory for the most part, but not without exceptions.

_____ 2. From 18-25, they're like South America:
Hot and exotic and ready to be explored.

_____ 3. From 25-30, they're like Asia:
Lots of history, but still places to go where no one has been.

_____ 4. From 30-45, they're like North America:
Fully explored, and exploiting their resources.

_____ 5. From 45-55, they're like Europe:
Exhausted, but wise, and with enough points of interest to make it worth the trip.

_____ 6. From 55 on, they're like Australia:
Everybody knows it's down there, but no one really gives a shit.

*

When do you know you're *really* drunk?

_____ 1. You sit down on a mop bucket and try to flush it!
_____ 2. The bathroom mirror is fogged, and you haven't turned the shower on yet!
_____ 3. You try to play a pizza on 33⅓!
_____ 4. You pull the car into the garage and tiptoe into the house, then realize that you live in an apartment!
_____ 5. You try to give a hickey to a snowman!
_____ 6. Somebody tells you to go fuck yourself and you ask them for the phone number!

*

Seven, Eight, Lay Them Straight!

Straight men are a very valuable commodity in show business, and here are a few commode ditties!

From the answers listed, fill in the proper straight line to complete the two-man joke.

Example:
Dick: I took my wife to Kansas City.
Peter: Did you get laid?
Dick: How could I get laid? My wife was with me!

Dick: I took my wife to the Islands.
Peter: _____?
Dick: No, she wanted to go!

Dick: Then we went to the Great Lakes.
Peter: _____?
Dick: Oh, she was pretty weird, yeah!

Dick: Then, I took her to Maine.
Peter: _____?
Dick: Of course!! She's my wife!

Dick: Then, we went to visit my cousin in Alaska.
Peter: _____?
Dick: Of *course* I know him!! He's my *cousin*!

Dick: Then, we went to Africa, where we played cards with the natives.
Peter: _____?
Dick: No, we mostly won.

Dick: I found out you can make a living as a comedian in Africa.
Peter: _____?
Dick: No, Ethiopia! Kenya has cable!

Dick: While we were in Africa, we shot a couple of monkeys, and I had them stuffed.

Peter: _____?

Dick: No, just shaking hands!

Responses:
a. Nassau
b. Portland
c. Zulus
d. Mounted
e. Jamaica
f. Nile
g. Why
h. Cannibals
i. Virgin
j. Nome
k. Erie
l. Bangor
m. Anchorage
n. Kenya
o. Basted
p. Bullshit

What's the eighties version of Kiss & Tell?

_____ 1. Shack and yak
_____ 2. Hose and disclose
_____ 3. Jab her and blabber
_____ 4. Tumble and rumble
_____ 5. Spurt and blurt
_____ 6. Go down and spread it around
_____ 7. Blow and show pictures

Which of the following was named *The Colorful Comparison of the Year* by the East Norwich Writer's Lodge in 1943?

____ 1. "As mixed up as a fart in a fan factory . . ."
____ 2. "As permanent as two flies fucking on a frog's fanny . . ."
____ 3. "As slick as snot on marble . . ."
____ 4. "Colder than a witch's tit in a brass bra . . ."
____ 5. "As busy as a one-armed paperhanger with an itchy nose . . ."
____ 6. "Tighter than a four-fingered glove . . ."
____ 7. "Cuter than a speckled pup goin' downhill in a red wagon . . ."
____ 8. "Crazier than a shithouse rat . . ."
____ 9. "As played out as 'go fuck yourself' in every multiple guess . . ."

*

Which of the following never had a snowball's chance in hell of being voted *The Most Sensitive Opening Line of a Song in the Sixties*?

____ 1. "Hey, birth control pill, now they all will, birth control pill . . ."
____ 2. "Bird drops keep falling on my head . . ."
____ 3. "Put your legs on my shoulder . . ."
____ 4. "She was just 51, and a helluva lot of fun, but the way she looked was way beyond repair . . ."
____ 5. "My boyfriend's black and my mother's gonna kill me . . ."
____ 6. "You don't remember me, but I remember you. Cause you got in my car with something on your shoe . . ."
____ 7. "You are my sunshine, my orange sunshine . . ."
____ 8. "Love . . . there's twenty-two of us . . ."

*

Which of the following questions was an obvious "yes" answer of the forties?

_____ 1. Did Pinocchio have a wooden willie?
_____ 2. Does a horny soldier cock his rifle?
_____ 3. Do Belgian Congo blowgun hunters dip their darts?
_____ 4. Does a nymphomaniac love every bone in her body?
_____ 5. Do babes with big bulbs get watts of attention?
_____ 6. Do gay sailors go down in submarines?
_____ 7. Does a crowded elevator smell different to a midget?
_____ 8. Did Gepetto pray every night for a son with a real penis?

*

What is the most obvious indication that a girl is getting too skinny?

_____ 1. She works in the library as a bookmark.
_____ 2. She can tap dance on Jell-O.
_____ 3. She can look through a keyhole with both eyes.
_____ 4. There's more meat on a busboy's vest.
_____ 5. She has to leave a movie because she can't hold the seat down.
_____ 6. She has to tease her hair to keep her pants up.
_____ 7. She hasn't got enough ass to keep her cunt off the sheet.

*

Build-A-Rankout

Using the beginning I have provided, construct the very best rankout, then use it for six or seven months until your friends start to twitch whenever they see it come to your lips. Then surprise them by not ever, *ever* changing it!

"I don't think you could get laid . . ."

_____ 1. ". . . if you crawled up a chicken's ass and waited your turn!"

_____ 2. ". . . in a bread line with a thirty-pound turkey!"

_____ 3. ". . . if you went into a whorehouse with a fistful of fifties and a tear in your eye!"

_____ 4. ". . . in a women's prison with a fistful of paroles!"

_____ 5. ". . . if I bought you a fuck-by-number set!"

Which of the following was rumoured to be *The Most Tasteless Bumper Sticker For A While*?

_____ 1. "Streakers beware! Your end is in sight!"

_____ 2. "*What* is a four-letter word!"

_____ 3. "Stamp out quicksand!"

_____ 4. "Greek style: scary at first, fun in the end!"

_____ 5. "Don't look for hand signals. The driver of this car is a convicted Arab shoplifter!"

_____ 6. "May the groundhog of happiness crawl into your hole!"

*

Which of the following is the best indication that your chubby child will grow up to be a porker of *unbelievable* proportions?

_____ 1. She was born an only twin.

_____ 2. You have to have her ears harpooned.

_____ 3. Department store Santas charge you time and a half.

_____ 4. His grammer school principal insures the seesaws.

_____ 5. Her hula hoop is skintight.

_____ 6. You go to a PTA meeting to petition to have phone booths let out.

_____ 7. She plays hopscotch on a tennis court.

_____ 8. He fits neat upon the seats of a bicycle built for two.

_____ 9. He finds money left under his pillow by the tusk fairy.

_____10. You take her to the Macy's parade and people look for her wires.

_____11. His first job is working at a sideshow as both sides.

_____12. The lower right-hand corner of her mirror says, "to be continued . . ."

_____13. He has to walk down the halls of his school sideways.

_____14. She needs a boomerang to throw a scarf around her neck.

_____15. Whenever he jumps in a hammock, the trees bump heads.

_____ 16. She sits on a Moped and you can't hear the engine.

*

Which of the following is the all-time best expression for making love?

_____ 1. Hauling the ashes

_____ 2. Poking

_____ 3. Laying pipe

_____ 4. Hiding the salami

_____ 5. Ramming home your pissing piston

_____ 6. Swapping gravy

_____ 7. Banging

_____ 8. Slipping the proverbial boneless ham

_____ 9. Porking

_____10. Putting on the fur collar

_____11. Bumping bellies

_____12. Making oink oink

_____13. Boffing

_____14. Going to Dallas

_____15. Fucking

*

Which of the following was *The Most Perverted Poem of 1969?*

A foolhardy midget named Fisher
Stuck his digit in The Fat Lady's fissure.
Her labial snap
Caught our boy in a trap.
Now they're fishing the fissure for Fisher!

A flatulent firper from Salem
Likes to loudly break wind, then inhale 'em.
Then he burps with delight!
A despicable sight!
But you don't need a bloodhound to trail him.

There once was a stud from Paree
Who went into an alley to pee.
He cried, "Sacre' bleu!
Ziss piss I can't do!!
I must have the C-L-A-P!"

Peter, Peter, pumpkin eater,
Had a wife and couldn't keep her.
Put her in a pumpkin shell,
And now that pumpkin smells like fish!

*

III.

Why did the Polish proctologist use two fingers? He wanted to get a second opinion!

How do you circumsize a woman?
Sit her naked on a wicker chair, and shave off whatever hangs down!

*

Who fucks for a fee in freshwater?
A prostitrout!

*

What would you call the prostitrout with the most seniority?
The oldest trick in the brook!

*

What's the first thing a sorority girl does in the morning?
Walks home!

*

What do you call it when a fag gets it in the ass from a donkey?
An enemule!

*

Why did the bald man have holes in his pockets?
He loved to run his fingers through his hair!

*

What's air pollution?
A fogging shame!

*

What's a happy Roman?
Gladiator!

*

What does it say on a black epileptic's medical bracelet?
"I'm not break dancing!"

*

How could you tell the fag was patriotic?
He wore red, white, and blew!

*

Why did they put a clock in the leaning tower of Pisa?
What good is the inclination if you haven't got the time?

*

What's the best way to get really stoned?
Drink wet cement!

*

The answer is eye strain. What's the question?
"What do you do when you can't afford a laxative?"

*

If a dried grape is a raisin, and a dried plum is a prune, what is
a dried cherry?
A nun!

*

What's the secret of a happy marriage?
The maid and the wife both come a couple of times a week!

*

What would you call a German bra?
Stoppenzumfrumfloppen!

*

What did the fisherman say to the magician?
"Take a cod, any cod!"

*

Why doesn't Billy Jean King shave her legs?
The hair holds up her sweat socks!

*

Why is money like manure?
It's no good unless you spread it around!

*

How can a baseball coach tell when his star player is in a severe slump?
He reaches to scratch himself and misses!

*

What did the Polish girl say when the gynecologist told her she had acute vaginitis??
"Thankyou!"

*

What cartoon character has weird eyes and blows Daddy Warbucks?
Little Oral Annie!

*

What's long and hard and excites a girl when she's finally lucky enough to get on it?
The road to success!

*

What was the ugly girl's job at the hospital?
To stand out front and make people sick!

What's the difference between grated manure and what a German calls his sweetheart?
Grated manure is *fine muck*!

*

Who has the world's smallest chicken coop?
A woman! There's only room for one cock, and he has to stand on his head to get in!

*

If a boxer wears boxer shorts, and a jockey wears jockey shorts, what would you call a guy that doesn't wear any shorts?
A swinger!

*

Why did the lights in the priest's motel room go off when the sexy girl walked in?
A willpower failure!

*

What's a vice squad?
A pussy posse!

*

What's the worst thing about playing softball in a cow pasture?
Sliding into what you thought was third base!

*

What's the difference between Grandma and a girl with her period?
Grandma goes to bed with *Gramps*!

*

Why do most luncheonettes close at five p.m.?
To let the soda jerk off!

*

Why were there so few Mexicans in the Olympics?
Because there was no burro-fucking competition!

*

What should you do if a girl gives you the slip?
Try to get the panties!

*

What's the deep freeze at the sperm bank?
A place whose come has time!

*

What do all animal lovers have in common?
Their habits are illegal!

*

Why do ugly girls hide on Ground Hog's Day?
Everybody's looking for a hog to grind up!

*

How is an erection like the theory of relativity?
The more you think about it, the harder it gets!

*

Who's the world's greatest actress?
A girl who can act naive on the first night of her second marriage!

*

What happened to the guy that banged the Eskimo woman?
He got chilled to the bone!

*

What happened to the owl that went in for a tonsillectomy and
developed hemorrhoids?
Now he can't hoot worth a shit or shit worth a hoot!

*

What's better for a girl than knowing what makes a man tick?
Knowing what makes him go off!

*

Why do jokes about oral sex choke people up?
Because they're in bad taste!

*

Why wasn't the girl sure if her date was going to be fun in bed?
Because he told her he'd be good for seconds!

*

What should you do if you feel strongly about graffiti?
Sign a partition!

*

Why did the kindergarten kid walk around with his zipper
open?
In case he had to count to eleven!

*

Why will there never be a shortage of horsemen?
They all like to ride bareback!

*

What do you call the emergency money a jogger keeps in his athletic supporter?
A trussed fund!

*

What did the lady game warden say to the fisherman?
"I hope you haven't got one under five inches!"

*

What are anecdotes about circle jerks?
Cock-and-pull stories!

*

Who's the most popular member of a horny softball team?
The designated hooker!

*

What's the national organization of herpes sufferers?
The American Lesion!

*

What's harder than getting a pregnant elephant in a Volkswagen?
Getting an elephant pregnant in a Volkswagen!

*

How can you tell the nearsighted man at the nudist colony?
It isn't hard!

*

What's a hump?
A noun meaning the thing on a camel's back, unless the thing is another camel, in which case it becomes a verb!

Who sells flowers in an outhouse?
A half-moonie!

*

How did Dolly Parton get her start?
In a jug band!

*

What does an impotent guy do on a waterbed?
The dead man's float!

*

What's an indication that a call girl is from a very small town?
The only thing open all night is her legs!

*

What's the difference between an alarm clock and a man's pecker?
The alarm clock goes *off* to get him *up*!

*

How is a woman like a toilet seat?
Without the hole in the middle, she wouldn't be good for shit!

*

What was the most outstanding feature of young Annette Funicello?
Her Mousketits!

*

What do you get when you cross a penis with a French fry?
A dictator!

*

Where does an Eskimo take a fat date?
Blubber's Lane!

*

If storks bring white babies, and crows bring black babies,
what kind of birds don't bring any babies?
No, not swallows! Woodpeckers!

*

What's the best way to keep people from stealing your Kotex?
Get a padlock!

*

What does the average husband fantasize when he's making
love?
That his wife isn't fantasizing!

*

When is it easiest for a man to have two orgasms?
When he's twins!

*

Why was the Polack looking for an archaeologist?
He found a used tampon and was wondering what period it was
from!

*

How can you keep from being bitten by a tsetse fly?
Keep your tsetse covered at all times!

*

Why should Linda Rondstadt try classical music next?
Because we'd all like to see her Bach side!

What did Dirty Johnny say when he caught his mother going down on his father?
"I can't believe you sent me to the psychiatrist for sucking on my *thumb*!"

*

What does a farmer call constipation?
Crap failure!

*

What's the worst thing about a leper giving you the finger?
Finding a place to keep it!

*

What's the best way to get excited?
Think hard!

*

Which college girls are the most fun?
The ones who think intercourse is the time between classes!

*

What was the headline when a lunatic escaped and went on a rampage attacking women?
"NUT BOLTS AND SCREWS!"

*

What would you call a sex-crazed clam?
A tramp steamer!

*

Why do blacks wear flared pants?
Because their knee grows!

What would you call a gay with the runs?
A juicy fruit!

*

Who are the only kids more screwed up than the kids whose
parents are divorced?
The kids whose parents stayed together!

*

What's the platform on The Prophylactic Party??
To limit production, stand up with inflation, allow room for
expansion, and to give the constituency a sense of security
while they're being screwed!

*

What would you call it if a group of Civil War amputees made
love to the same nurse?
A gangrene bang!

*

Why do horny men make lousy bank robbers?
After they pull their wives panty hose over their heads, they
wind up jumping back in bed with them!

*

How did the dachshund meet his end?
Running around a tree!

*

What happened to the fashion conscious girl who had five sets
of tits?
She wound up on The Ten Breast Dressed List!

*

What happens if a man swallows an aphrodisiac too slowly?
He gets a stiff neck!

*

What would you call a shack where gays meet on weekends??
A bunghole boffing bungalow!!

*

What would you call a constipated Chinaman?
Hung Chow!

*

Why does everybody masturbate?
Because we all know that if you want something done right,
you have to do it yourself!

*

Why doesn't Howard Cosell clean out his ears?
His head would cave in!

*

What did the family rename their cat Ben after she gave birth to
ten kittens?
Ben Hur!

*

What's the difference between a diaphragm and diarrhea?
A diaphragm *keeps* out the squirts; diarrhea *creeps* out the
squirts!

*

What do you get when an A-bomb explodes in the kitchen?
Linoleum blownapart!

Why is it all right for a son to go into debt for his father?
Because his father went into the hole for him!

*

What would you call a sex party where everybody falls asleep?
A snorgy!

*

What's the difference between an optimist and a pessimist on
their wedding nights?
The optimist hears, "That's happiness . . .", and the pessimist hears, "*That's a penis?*"

*

What was the only song ever written about pajamas?
Torn Between Love and Duty!

*

What's a virgin?
A girl that whispers sweet nothing-doings in your ear!

*

What's the most important thing in a sexual relationship?
Complete honesty. Once you learn to fake that, you've got it
made!

*

What do we know about the fellow that first said, "Time heals
all wounds?"
He wasn't aware of herpes or pussy!

*

What does a man do standing up, a woman sitting down, and a dog on three legs?
Shake hands!

*

What did the fag say as he shoved a baloney up his lover's ass?
"The wurst is yet to come!"

*

What happened when Ronald Reagan ran a red light?
He broke his nose on a whorehouse door!

*

What would you call an Eskimo girl's twat?
A chatterbox!

*

What part of a girl does a man most enjoy watching?
The top of her head!

*

What do we realize when we learn Ben Franklin had 33 illigitimate children?
That his kite wasn't all that stayed up!
(He was one of our pounding fathers!)

*

What was the x-rated version of *Poor Richard's Almanac*?
Tired Dick's Diary!

*

What's the sexiest four-letter word?
Cash!

What do you get when you cross a pickle and a deer?
A dill doe!

*

What's something singer Vic Damone can never do?
Wear monogrammed shirts!

*

Why can't Richard Pryor and Eddie Murphy get into the Friar's Club?
They're black-balled!

*

What's an indication that a homosexual is very promiscuous?
His ass is so stretched it has a drawstring!

*

Why is it ridiculous for women to complain that men make love too fast?
How much speed can you build up in 45 seconds?

*

Why is it estimated that only 99% of all people masturbate?
The other 1% were either taking the poll or answering the door!

*

How do you get 100 Cubans into a shoe box?
Tell them it floats!

*

What's a vampire's favorite kind of music?
Ragtime!

*

What would you call the zipper on a gay Italian's pants?
A Mediterranean fruit fly!

*

What's the main difference between men and women?
Women must play hard to get; men must get hard to play!

*

What happened when the little boy fell in the vat of gum?
His mother chewed him out!

*

Why does an orthodox Jewish girl wear a bikini?
To separate the meat from the milk!

*

What did the patriot say as an excuse when he couldn't get
excited because his wife had her period?
"Better dead than red!"

*

What do you get when you put LSD in your cornflakes?
Breakfast surreal!

*

Why can't congressmen keep up with their work?
They're always behind a page or two!

*

What happened when Bob Guccione ran naked pictures of
Vanessa Williams in *Penthouse*?
We saw her end as Miss America!

*

What would you call an exhibitionist in an insane asylum?
Flip flash!

*

What has four legs and eats ants?
Two uncles!

*

Why did the Warsaw aquarium close down?
The clam drowned!

*

Why did Dolly Parton's teeth fall out?
Her dentist couldn't reach them!

*

What would you call a gay S&M bar in Massachusetts?
Kickingham and Stickingham!

*

How did the owner show that his dog was a blacksmith?
He held a lit match under the dog's balls, and the dog made a
bolt for the door!

*

How did the psychiatrist diagnose the patient that complained
of one day feeling like a teepee, and the next day feeling like a
wigwam?
Too tense!

*

What was the world's grossest movie?
The Texas Chain Saw Vasectomy!

What did the girl say about her boyfriend who was very fond of anal sex?
"With friends like him, who needs enemas?"

*

What's a redneck?
A guy who'll fuck a black girl, but won't go to school with her!

*

What nationality is Santa Claus?
North Polish!

*

What's one thing you should never do in a San Francisco theatre?
Ask someone to hold your seat!

*

What is the single most obnoxious thing a Jewish American Princess has ever done?
Hired a schwartze to come in every couple of weeks and pick the cotton out of the medicine bottles!

*

What's a hen?
A cock without a cock!

*

What do you get when an epileptic falls into the lettuce patch?
Seizure salad!

*

What's the best way to part a girl's hair?
With your tongue!

Why did the T.V. programmer go to the doctor for another enema prescription?
He had the reruns!

*

How do gays rationalize their preference?
"It's just pussy on a stick!"

*

Where does a vampire soak himself?
In the bat tub!

*

How can you tell a neighborhood has a serious drug problem?
Elementary school children are snorting cocaine flavor candy straws!

*

What's this: "VVRRrroom! RRRrrtt! VVRRrroom! RRRrrtt!?"
A Polack trying to drive through a blinking red light!

*

How did the sadistic nurse punish her patient?
She dipped his rectal thermometer in Ben-Gay!

*

Why is sex so universal?
Because everybody fucks in the same language!

*

How can you tell the Irish guy in the hospital ward?
He's the one blowing the foam off his bedpan!

*

Why is life worth living?
There's nothing else you can do with it!

*

What would you call a vampire in drag?
A transylvestite!

*

Why do madams prefer one-story brothels?
So there'll be no fucking overhead!

*

How are angry apartment neighbors like houseflies?
They bang on the wall!

*

What happened after the cannibal schoolboy ate all his classmates?
He passed the third grade!

*

What did the waiter say when his customer announced that the lady he was with was drinking Budweiser??
"Anheuser Busch?"

*

What's the difference between a male robot and a female robot?
Lug nuts!

*

How do you know when your girlfriend has emitted an incredible fart?
You hear it, even though you're in the kitchen popping popcorn and she's upstairs *in the bathtub*!

Why did the Polack have to close his topless restaurant in the middle of business hours?
It started to rain!

*

What's the most common reaction you get when you tell two people they look alike?
They both get pissed off!

*

What should you use to fuck a lady genie?
A wishbone!

*

What kind of soup does a fag order in a Chinese restaurant?
Cream of sum yung guy!

*

What's a birth control pill?
The other thing a girl can put in her mouth to keep from getting pregnant!

*

What would you call a kosher tampon?
Tightwad!

*

Why did the cannibal overcook the only mind reader he had ever captured??
He wanted his rare medium well-done!

*

What's the difference between a male exhibitionist and a female exhibitionist?
His point of view!

*

Why should you fuck a mountain goat on the edge of a cliff?
So you'll be sure she pushes back!

*

What should you do if you find an epileptic in your bathtub?
Throw in your laundry and two cups of Tide!

*

What does every man have that gets bigger if you stroke it?
An ego!

*

What is modern pussy?
Cuntemporary!

*

What did Benny Hill answer when The Queen asked him if he wanted to have some tea in her private chamber?
"A cup would be just fine, mum!"

*

What's a coolie?
A quickie in the snow!

*

What does a fag call a guy that sticks a ballpoint up his ass?
A pen pal!

*

What's a hula hoop with a nail in it?
A navel destroyer!

*

What starts with "c", ends with "t", and means the same as pussy?
Cat!

*

How did the Germans conquer Poland?
They marched in backwards and said they were leaving!

*

What's a poor man's Jacuzzi?
Farting in the bathtub!

*

What would you call a farmboy that won't fuck cows?
A non-dairy creamer!

*

What does Prince Charles have for breakfast?
An English muff!

*

What happened to the Polack that put a mirror over his bed?
He didn't do any better with the women, but it cured his coke habit!

*

What goes "ha ha ha thump!"
A leper laughing his head off!

*

What's a degenerate?
Someone who can't afford to hide his vices!

*

What's a minute man?
A guy who double parks in front of a whorehouse!

*

What would you call a rabbit with the crabs?
Bugs bunny!

*

What do you call congressional aides who are into golden showers?
The yellow pages!

*

What did George Washington say to his men before they got into the boat?
"Men, get in the boat!"

*

What would you call a medieval masturbator?
A pounding serf!

*

What's the worst thing a doctor can do when you call him and tell him you're constipated?
Put you on hold!

*

What's the difference between a razor and a Greek that works for Mayflower Van Lines?
One is a hair remover, and the other is a hairy mover!

How were Moses's parents doubly blessed?
They not only had fun in bed, but they made a prophet!

*

What do they serve at an Italian leper colony?
Elbow macaroni!

*

What would you call a hernia on a sea lion?
A loose seal ball!

*

What did the boss say when one of his employees said he'd like
to take the day off to attend his mother-in-law's funeral?
"Who wouldn't?"

*

How can you tell if a bear is gay?
He lays his paw on the table!

*

Who was probably the first person to declare masturbation
perfectly normal?
Someone who was *very* normal!

*

What would you call Siamese twins with no arms and no legs?
Matched potatoes!

*

Why is it so much fun to take a fat girl to a country-western
bar?
Because you can get drunk and play the washboard on her
chins!

What's the reason a lot of couples don't 69?
They never get around to it!

*

What did the Polack do when his girlfriend asked him to do something kinky?
Shit in her purse!

*

What's a wife?
An attachment you screw on the bed to get the housework done!

*

Why do so many guys come back from the bathroom with wet spots on the front of their pants?
Because their peckers can't snort!

*

When should parents suspect that their teenager has a coke habit?
If his pet rock is from Bolivia!

*

What do they bring you when you want to order food in a lesbian bar?
A womenu!

*

What should you do if your date says it's nice out?
Leave it out!

*

What do you get when you cross a turkey with an ostrich?
A bird with huge drumsticks that keeps burying his head in the mashed potatoes!

*

What do you get when you cross a kleptomaniac with a nymphomaniac?
A fuckin' thief!!

*

When does a girl win playing strip poker?

_____ 1. When douches are wild
_____ 2. When someone slips her an inside straight
_____ 3. If all the guys wind up in the hole
_____ 4. If she has a nice pair
_____ 5. If she raises all the men
_____ 6. If she deals all the men down and dirty
_____ 7. If she has to ask the guys one by one, "Are you in?"
_____ 8. If she knows enough to not hold on to queens
_____ 9. All of the above

*

When do you know a girl is really ugly?

_____ 1. She has to pester Hare Krishnas for pamphlets.
_____ 2. She makes your dick go back in like a turtle.
_____ 3. You take her to a flea circus and she steals the show.
_____ 4. The only person that can talk to her is Dr. Doolittle.
_____ 5. You don't know whether to shake her hand or sniff her ass.
_____ 6. She looks like she got halfway through a sex change and ran out of money.
_____ 7. Cops pull her over and tell her to speed up.

*

Of all colorful expressions, none seem to gather as fast as those for the good old fart. Which of the following is the best of the new crop?

____ 1. Bowel howl
____ 2. Cushion creeper
____ 3. Bucksnorter
____ 4. Paint the elevator
____ 5. Blinky
____ 6. Skivvie sniffle
____ 7. Boomer
____ 8. Rattle the fudge
____ 9. Breeze lunch
____10. Whiffle
____11. Crunch a plastic cup
____12. Bronx honk
____13. Poot
____14. Beanie
____15. House frog
____16. Boopse

*

Which of the following is the best clue that a girl is a huge, overstuffed bimbo?

____ 1. She stores her dildo in a silo.
____ 2. She can dance cheek to cheek with herself.
____ 3. People hang glide off her tits.
____ 4. After she walks down an aisle in corduroys, they make her sit in the smoking section.
____ 5. Her shaft has a draft.
____ 6. She has to kick start her vibrator.
____ 7. Her proctologist is a member of The United Mine Workers.
____ 8. She looks like the Liberty Bell, only her crack is bigger.
____ 9. She's built so low to the ground, every time she farts she blows sand into her shoes.
____10. When you have sex with her, it's like walking through a warm room with your fly open.

Old Comedians Never Stop Pounding Away, Their Fans Just Stop Coming!
Complete the jokes with the answers across the page!

Example:
"Old fishermen never die . . ."
". . . they just stop reaching for their flies . . ."

_____ 1. "Old queers never die . . ."
_____ 2. "Old bullfrogs never die . . ."
_____ 3. "Old firemen never die . . ."
_____ 4. "Old postmen never die . . ."
_____ 5. "Old radio announcers never die . . ."
_____ 6. "Old hockey players never die . . ."
_____ 7. "Old auto inspectors never die . . ."
_____ 8. "Old truckers never die . . ."
_____ 9. "Old golfers never die . . ."
_____10. "Old rabbis never die . . ."
_____11. "Old generals never die . . ."
_____12. "Old sea captains never die . . ."
_____13. "Old palace guards never die . . ."
_____14. "Old songwriters never die . . ."

_____a. ". . . they just lose their frequency!"

_____b. ". . . they just have expired stickers!"

_____c. ". . . they just can't keep their privates at attention!"

_____d. ". . . they just croak!"

_____e. ". . . they just roll up their hoses and move on to a new flame!"

_____f. ". . . they just can't cut it anymore!"

_____g. ". . . they just can't keep their logs up!"

_____h. ". . . they just decompose!"

_____i. ". . . they just blow away!"

_____j. ". . . they just stop standing out in front!"

_____k. ". . . they just lose their zip!"

_____l. ". . . they just get a new Peterbilt!"

_____m. ". . . they just lose their balls!"

_____n. ". . . they just get too cold to puck around anymore!"

_____o. ". . . they just go fuck themselves!"

*

111

Encore!
Which of the following is *not* the actual punch line to a classic joke?

___ 1. "Oui, Monsieur, and in three or four days, you vill haf a rash! You may call it measles!"
___ 2. "What? And quit show business?"
___ 3. "Why don't you just throw it over your shoulder and go as a gasoline pump?"
___ 4. "Just like I said, you weren't so 'ot! You were in such a rush, you 'ad a bit o' me scarf tucked in!"
___ 5. "You know, Myrtle, you seen one, you seen 'em all, but this one's eating my popcorn!"
___ 6. "Thanks anyway, but if ten won't kill the taste, I don't think one more is gonna help!"

*

Which of the following was proclaimed *Religious Bumper Sticker Of The Year, 1982*?

___ 1. "Virtue is its own punishment"
___ 2. "Keep New York Clean! Eat A Pigeon!"
___ 3. "Grass is Mother Nature's way of saying Hi!"
___ 4. "Life is hard, then you die"
___ 5. "I choked Linda Lovelace!"
___ 6. "Whale Oil Beef Hooked!"

*

Which of the following is the best new expression for a male homosexual?

___ 1. Poof
___ 2. Fly squatter
___ 3. Meathead
___ 4. Bishop browner
___ 5. Tonsil hockey teddy
___ 6. Heinie climber
___ 7. Tinker bell

*

Which of the following do *you* consider to be the funniest, most creative name for a male burlesque dancer from the United Kingdom?

_____ 1. Miles O'Toole
_____ 2. Big Ben
_____ 3. The Scotland Yard
_____ 4. Jack the Stripper
_____ 5. His Majesty the Dink of England
_____ 6. Wingo Starr
_____ 7. Baggy Pipes
_____ 8. Milt the Kilt and his Wilted Stilt
_____ 9. Dublin Peter
_____10. Big Mac and his Quarter Pounder
_____11. Marty Python

*

Which of the following is considered by most of Westchester County and parts of Juarez, Mexico, to be the most often heard expression for a girl menstruating?

_____ 1. Having her period
_____ 2. El pussita siesta
_____ 3. Has her friend
_____ 4. Jammin'
_____ 5. On the rag
_____ 6. Straddling the canoe
_____ 7. So solly, no fuckee
_____ 8. Sittin' on shark bait

*

Which of the following award-winning similes was awarded the highest honors at the legendary Gershon Legman's First Erotic Luncheon in Valbonne, France, in 1964?

_____ 1. "As funny as a clumsy nurse with a full bed-pan . . ."
_____ 2. "As anxious as the center on a Fire Island football team . . ."
_____ 3. "As welcome as poison ivy at a nudist colony picnic . . ."
_____ 4. "Drier than a terrier on a tree farm . . ."
_____ 5. "As strong as stud horse piss with the foam farted off . . ."
_____ 6. "As pure as the driven slush . . ."
_____ 7. "As honest as a Chinese redhead . . ."
_____ 8. "As stoned as a Jamaican housewife . . ."
_____ 9. "Closer than Siamese faggots . . ."
_____10. "As fishy as a mermaid's megumbo . . ."

*

Which of the following has been hailed by everyone from rodeo cowboys to masochistic athletes as the expression for condom that most people don't know?

_____ 1. Coney Island whitefish
_____ 2. Bag
_____ 3. Rubber deuter twister
_____ 4. Baby blocking baggie
_____ 5. Safe
_____ 6. Bedroom slipcover
_____ 7. Trojan
_____ 8. Go fuck someone

*

Which of the following was *The Best Opening Line of a Song in the Forties?*

_____ 1. "Beautiful dreamer, wake under me.
You shouldn't snooze while we're making woo-pee . . ."
_____ 2. "Oh, how we danced on the night we were wed.
Oh, how we danced, 'cause the room had no bed . . ."
_____ 3. "By the sea, by the sea, by the C-U-N-T . . ."
_____ 4. "If you knew Susie, like I know Susie, you'd need some of this lotion, too . . ."
_____ 5. "I'll be seeing you in all the oiled familiar places . . ."

*

1938's Lewdest Limerick of the Year was:

At Bud's wedding he got quite a fright.
The bride's old man got very tight.
With his twenty-first beer,
He burped in Bud's ear,
"Would you like to swap wives for tonight?"

Roses are red, violets are purple,
I dig your titties by the slurpful!
(This was disqualified. Not because it's not a limerick, but because it was written by a member of the family of the contest's sponsor)

A horny young stud from Cape Ann
Likes to grind his girl's ass in the sand.
When the gnats are about,
He won't pull it out,
Which accounts for the bites on his can!

There was a young man from Arras
Who stretched himself out on the grass,
And with no little trouble,
Bent himself double,
And stuck his prick well up his ass!

115

After careful research and much alcoholic recreation, which of the following has our team of jag-offs determined to be well on its way to becoming *The Absolute Worst Opening Line of the Eighties*?

_____ 1. "Can I buy you a car?"
_____ 2. "Big deal, Spielberg makes a million a day. You're here talking to me!"
_____ 3. "Want to go sunbathing tonight?"
_____ 4. "I hope you feel as good as you smell."
_____ 5. "You hereby have squatter's rights to my face!"
_____ 6. "I won't tell you I have a monstrous cock because I know for a fact that doesn't matter to you guys . . ."

*

IV.

What should you brush with after oral sex?
Douche paste!

Why did Johnny think that his father had two dicks?
Because he saw him use a small one to pee, and a huge one to brush the babysitter's teeth!

*

Why was the faggot smiling when they released him from jail in the morning?
He had spent the night in the can!

*

What was the Marx Brothers' ugly sister's name?
Alpo!

*

What would you call a guy that takes a tinkle on the third rail?
A conductor!

*

How do we know girls aren't made of sugar and spice?
They taste like anchovies!

*

What would you call a girlfriend who does your shirts for you?
An ironing broad!

*

What's the worst thing about fucking a video game?
When the list appears on the screen of all the guys that have done better!

*

Which maids are the best in bed?
The ones that can change mop handles with their hands tied behind their backs!

*

Where do shady boogers come from?
The Shadow Nose!

*

Why are animal jokes so confusing?
If a sheep is a ram and a mule is an ass, how come a ram in the ass is a goose?

*

What's a Fire Island vampire?
A clot sucker!

*

Why aren't there any Polish cheerleaders?
Because every time they do a split, either the grass dies or the floor buckles!

*

What would you call a guy with no arms or legs in a vat of beer?
Bud!

*

Why don't all women make split pea soup?
Because some men prefer to eat the pea whole!

*

When is giving head like eating watermelon?
When you spit out the seeds!

119

What's the best way to have group sex if you're shy?
Fuck a schizo!

*

What's a T.V. censor?
A bleeping tom!

*

What did the girl say after she accidentally grabbed the Krazy Glue instead of the KY Jelly?
"My lips are sealed!"

*

What do cannibals make from politicians?
Baloney sandwiches!

*

What happened when three guys jumped a girl in a San Francisco park?
Two of them held her down and the third one did her hair!

*

What did one frog say to the other frog?
"Time sure is fun when you're having flies!"

*

Why is a tampon like a Jewish American Princess?
They're both stuck up cunts!

*

What's worse than a joke about shit?
A joke about shit that's corny!

*

What do biker chicks have tattooed on the top of their heads?
"Let go of my ears! I know what I'm doing!"

*

What goes "peck, peck, bang!?"
A chicken in a mine field!

*

What's the definition of a tough guy?
A guy who bangs his dick against the side of the urinal to dry it off!

*

What's the best way to keep your friends?
Don't give them away!

*

Where did the Jewish cannibal go?
To a cafeteria that advertised "children half price!"

*

Why can't gays get car insurance?
They get rear-ended too often!

*

What happened to the girl who bent over in tight slacks?
She got a split in her pants and pants in her split!

*

Why don't Frenchmen buy tomato slicers?
Because they like to eat their tomatoes whole!

*

121

How do you know when you're really wrecked on quaaludes?
Somebody tells you to go fuck yourself and it sounds like a good idea!

*

Why don't Polacks wear short-sleeved shirts?
It would be disgusting to wipe snot on their bare wrists!

*

What sound does a urologist's watch make?
Dick doc!

*

What do you get when you cross a rabbit with a Ubangi?
A jungle bunny with a harelip!

*

What would you call a girl who drops her pants every time a man drops a hint?
A suggestion box!

*

Why was the street cleaner fired?
He couldn't keep his mind in the gutter!

*

What do you get when you give a blind man an enema?
A No. 2 pencil!

*

Why did the Polish girl wring out her nightgown on the counter at the sperm bank?
It was a deposit slip!

*

How are old men like bumper stickers?
They're hard to get off!

*

What does an alcoholic with one leg drink?
Hop scotch!

*

What's a 71?
69 with two fingers in someone's ass!

*

What do you get when you cross marijuana with an aphrodisiac?
Tumbleweed!

*

What's a sexual hangup?
The hook you hang your douche bag from!

*

How did the seagulls know they were flying over a "ship of fools"?
The people were looking up!

*

How can you tell if a gay is going on a diet?
He has his throat fitted for a diaphragm!

*

What's the best thing to give your date for dessert?
A creme-filled Ding Dong!

*

What does a Jewish American Princess have to do before she has plastic surgery?
Go to the doctor's office and pick her nose!

*

What's a babysitter?
A teenage girl you hire to make out with her boyfriend on the couch while your child cries itself to sleep!

*

What did the woman mutter as she crawled through the desert with her douche bag?
"Vinegar and water . . . I need vinegar and water . . ."

*

What's the definition of a crummy bastard?
A little boy eating crackers in church while his parents are getting married!

*

Why do tampons have strings?
So you can floss after you eat!

*

Why is being in the service like getting a blowjob?
The closer you get to discharge, the better you feel!

*

What does a rabbi play on the piano?
Chops dicks!

*

What happened to the girl that had an imaginary friend?
She was sent to the State Menstrual Institution for an indefinite period!

What did the Polack say when the urologist asked him if his pecker burned after intercourse?
"I don't know, Doc, I've never tried to light it!"

*

When does the Greek flag fly at half-mast?
When it gets pushed there!

*

What did Speedy Gonzales say to the virgin?
"It won't hurt, did it?"

*

Why are turds tapered at the ends?
So your asshole won't slam shut!

*

Why did the Polack spray his dick with Right Guard?
He was going on a date and wanted 8-hour protection!

*

What's the AAAAA?
An organization for people that are being driven to drink!

*

How do you circumsize a leper?
Shake him!

*

What did the bartender whisper to the lesbian when the bull dyke walked into the bar?
"She's hung like a doughnut!"

*

What's the Dog's Rule Of Life?
"If you can't eat it or fuck it, piss on it!"

*

What kind of tourists are the most fun?
Clit-tourists!

*

What would you call a large fish sandwich at McDonald's?
A quarter flounder!

*

How can you tell if a girl has just had sex with an elephant?
She sits on a barstool and sinks to the floor!

*

What does a young Indian do if he has no date to take to the war party?
Beats his tom-tom!

*

What would you call a bi-sexual prehistoric comic strip character?
A.C.D.C.B.C.!

*

What do you call it when three college guys get stoned in a dormitory room and imagine they have dates?
A mirage a' trois!

*

What did they call Sex Ed. in the fifties?
Recess!

How did *A Tale of Two Titties* begin?
"It was the bust of times . . ."

*

What's bed rheumatism?
Your joint *won't* get stiff!

*

If you met a girl in Chicago and she told you she gave the best head in town, what should you pay her?
A visit!

*

How can a guy tell he had a great date?
When he wakes up in the morning and his face feels like a glazed doughnut!

*

What's the difference between beer nuts and deer nuts?
Beer nuts are a dollar and a quarter; deer nuts are under a buck!

*

How can you keep your relatives away?
Borrow from the rich ones and loan it to the poor ones, and you'll never see any of them again!

*

Who jerked off during The Revolutionary War?
John Handcock!

*

What's a person who's into golden showers?
A pea nut!

What would you call a guy with no arms or legs who gets attacked by a lion?
Claude!

*

Why did the young bride have mixed emotions regarding having just tied the knot?
Because, after three weeks of married life, she felt like a new woman . . . but so did her husband!

*

What happened to the leper in New York City?
Someone stole her kneecaps!

*

Why wouldn't the female spy give the CIA agent head unless he wore a condom?
She wanted to blow his cover!

*

Why did the Manhattan fag move to Long Island?
So he could be listed in the Queens Directory!

*

What is experience?
Something that enables you to recognize a mistake when you make it again!

*

What's the difference between a snake and a goose?
A snake is an *asp* in the *grass*!

*

How do you prepare kidney beans?
Cook the piss out of them!

*

How did the teenage boy get a cracked vertebra?
He was kissing his girlfriend goodnight on the back porch when her father walked out and stepped on his back!

*

Where does Deuphus, god of retarded children, live?
Mount Special Olympus!

*

What's the toughest thing about being endowed like Dolly Parton?
Going through most of your life being the last one to know what's on your fork!

*

What's the difference between mashed potatoes and pea soup?
You can mash potatoes!

*

What's an M&M love affair?
You take in a meal and a movie before you melt in her mouth, *not* in her hand!

*

Why were the three fraternity brothers all trying to impress a girl they knew had herpes?
They were competing for her infection!

*

What did the nymphomaniac do when the basketball team bus broke down in front of her house?
She put 'em all up!

*

What were the results when the Polack tried getting some of his underarm hair transplanted to his bald head?
It was the pits!

*

What do you get when you cross a cat with a rabbit?
Pussy hares!

*

What did the guy do when he realized his wife had her panties on backwards?
He chewed her ass out!

*

Why don't alcoholics order cokes at Burger King?
They always have the shakes!

*

What would you call a depressed whale penis?
Mopey Dick!

*

Why shouldn't a girl be upset after she loses her cherry?
She's still got the box it came in!

*

What kind of song is *Come Fill My Cuspidor*?
A spit tune!

Who invented the bagpipes?
The Irish! Then, as a goof, they gave it to the Scottish and told them it was a musical instrument!

*

Why did the leper pitcher retire?
He threw his arm out!

*

What's a good indication to a wife that her husband had a wild night?
She finds a false eyelash in his pubic hair!

*

What do you have to know to be a plumber?
Shit doesn't go uphill and don't bite your fingernails!

*

What happened to the man who married the woman of his dreams?
He woke up fast!

*

What happens if you drink white wine with fish?
The fish get rude and belligerent!

*

Why do women have bellybuttons?
So men will have a place to put their gum on the way down!

*

What did the priest say when he walked into his hotel room and found two naked women??
"Out! Out! One of you will have to get out!"

What do fat women do in the summer?
Stink!

*

When is spanking permitted in public schools?
Between consenting teachers!

*

What does a girl make with her vibrator?
Fake snake soup!

*

Why are psychiatrists a waste of time?
They find you cracked and leave you broke!

*

What's the best way to make a bull sweat?
Put him in a tight jersey!

*

Why didn't the Polish girl think she gave good head?
Because she couldn't get her lips all the way over her boyfriend's ears!

*

What's the swinger's version of love at first sight?
Thrust at first lust!

*

What would you call a fag without AIDS?
One lucky cocksucker!

*

What would you call a guy with no arms, no legs, and no torso?
Dick!

*

What do you know if your camel steak is too salty?
It's from the hump!

*

What's an indication that the pilot flying your airplane is very young?
He comes on the intercom and starts telling you what he did over his summer vacation!

*

What's brown and full of holes?
Swiss shit!

*

What do you call an erection you get from smoking opium?
Poppy cock!

*

What would you call a chain of Polish convenience stores?
"Pick And Eat It!"

*

What's a gay cannibal?
A headhunter!

*

What did King Kong say to Zsa Zsa Gabor?
"Is it in?"

What's the difference between a straight guy and a gay guy?
When something goes up a straight guy's ass, there's usually a fingernail on it!

*

What's more important to a woman than the men in her life?
The life in her men!

*

Why did the midget peeping tom decide to become a ballet dancer?
Because he had so much experience standing on his toes!

*

How did the pregnant dentist find out the sex of the child she was carrying?
She used the metal thing with the little mirror on the end!

*

Why did God give Italians arms?
So their fingers wouldn't smell like their armpits!

*

Why is marriage like a bath?
Once you get used to it, it ain't so hot!

*

Where's the worst place for teenagers to get their braces locked?
On their girlfriends' I.U.D.'s!

*

What's the best way to kiss a girl's bellybutton?
From the inside!

What movie star banged underage girls in the forties but didn't get anybody pregnant?
Sterile Flynn!

*

Where do all the Alpine pansies come from?
Swisherland!

*

What was it when the Supreme Court judge pushed his pregnant girlfriend down the stairs?
A miscarriage of justice!

*

What's worse than biting into an apple and finding a worm?
Finding half a worm!

*

What was the public's reaction to the news that the board of directors of The Miss America Beauty Pageant were all down on Vanessa Williams?
Most of us hoped that *Penthouse* got a few shots of that, too!

*

What's an indication your wife is getting nearsighted?
You wake up and she's sucking on the bedpost!

*

What did George and Gracie call their act when they had the clap?
Burns and Itches!

*

What happens in the x-rated version of King Kong?
He climbs on the Statue of Liberty!

How do you tell someone to eat shit in Chinese?
"Moo goo bed pan!"

*

What's a Polish stud's opening line?
"You smell like you want to be alone!"

*

What does a guy have that's six inches long and proves he's a man?
His birth certificate!

*

What would you call a girl with three boobs and two pussies?
A smorgasbroad!

*

Why was it obvious that Pia Zadora was bombing in the lead role of the stage version of "The Diary Of Anne Frank"?
Because when the German soldiers came to the door, the entire audience yelled, "She's in the attic!"

*

What's the difference between a bad husband and a good husband?
A bad husband *boxes* his wife's *jaws*!

*

Why do women have their two holes so close together?
So if they pass out drunk, you can carry them home like a six-pack!

*

What should you do if a moonie is drowning?
Throw him an anchor!

*

What are blueballs?
A vice to the love lorn!

*

Why is a metal coffin preferable to a wooden coffin?
Because if you buy a wooden coffin, in a couple of months
you'll be out on your ass!

*

What's soft, fuzzy, and the most fun when it's going up and
down?
A mink yo-yo!

*

Why is the chicken farmer who invented the huge machine that
automatically separates the chicken fillets from the skeletons so
proud?
He's got the biggest boner on the East Coast!

*

What's a hum job?
Choral sex!

*

What happens to elephants when they use sheep for tampons?
They get Toxic Flock Syndrome!

*

What did the horny girl on her way downtown to see her boyfriend do when she got caught in traffic?
Found an alternate root!

*

How does a Polack get the stains off his undies?
Pulls them over his head and shouts them out!

*

A man died, and when he came to, he had a keg of beer next to him and a beautiful girl on his lap. How did he know he was in Hell?
There was a hole in the bottom of the keg and none in the bottom of the girl!

*

Can you catch VD on a toilet seat?
Yes, but it's very uncomfortable, especially for the person on the bottom!

*

What's grosser than your grandfather getting a boner while you're sitting on his lap?
Your grandmother lifting her dress up and saying, "Come on, kids, we're eating out tonight!"

*

What did the three-legged dog say as he moseyed into the bar out West?
"I'm lookin' for the man who shot my paw!"

*

When does a mother feel she's a failure?
When her son sweeps the streets her daughter walks!

Who was the first frankfurter entrepeneur?
Eve! She made Adam's hot dog stand!

*

What should a woman do if she doesn't like the way her son dresses?
Stop watching him!

*

What's an indication that your date is frigid?
You lick her thigh and your tongue sticks to her leg!

*

What's the difference between a mother-in-law and a bucket of shit?
The bucket!

*

What goes "Nort! Nort!?"
A bull with a hare lip!

*

Who wears space panties?
Girls who think their asses are out of this world!

*

What's a shotgun wedding?
A case of wife or death!

*

How is the recent crab research progressing?
They're just starting to scratch the surface!

*

Why did the teenage girl blame her pregnancy on her mother?
Because her mother had never taught her how to give a decent
blowjob!

*

What would a guy call his partner if she had a real bad acne
problem?
His main squeeze!

*

What's the best thing to do if you like home cooking?
Eat your girlfriends!

*

What happened to the guy's sex life after he accidentally
dropped a quarter, two dimes, and a nickel into his wife's
pussy?
He could feel the change!

*

What sees purple and launches flying saucers?
A tripping waiter!

*

What canarial disease do birds get from flocking around with
carrier pigeons?
Chirpees!! And there's no tweetment!

*

When does sitting in front of a fire with your date cease to be
romantic?
When the trucks get there!

*

How did the pretty young girl get a break in show business?
Obviously, she was on the right face at the right time!

*

What happens when a foxy girl goes wading in the ocean?
The herrings get hard-ons!

*

What's a female voyeur?
A peeping tomboy!

*

What does it say on the first page of a Polish sex manual?
"The cunt is in the front!"

*

What's a Greek wet dream?
Shits that pass in the night!

*

Who was Groucho's fat sister?
Stretch Marx!

*

Why was the traveling salesman starving?
The only thing he had had in his mouth all day were a whore's
tongue and a toothbrush!

*

Why did the girl break up with the mentalist?
He didn't care about her body; all he wanted her for was her
mind!

*

Why did the Polack quit his job as washroom attendant?
He couldn't figure out how to refill the electric hand dryer!

*

Why don't teddy bears make any noise when they screw?
They have cotton balls!

*

What happened to the tomboy who was stranded at a station with seven commuters?
She wound up pulling the train!

*

Which of the following snappy retorts would you consider the best ammunition for a young lady who is posed the old question, "Do you go all the way?"

____ 1. "No, but my brother does. Bring your mother around!"
____ 2. "That depends. How long is the ride?"
____ 3. "No, but I'll open the gates while you do!"
____ 4. "Yeah, and you can't come!"
____ 5. "That depends. How long is your root?"
____ 6. "Stick your dick in your nose and beat it!"
____ 7. "Go fuck yourself!"
____ 8. "I didn't until just now, you silver-tongued box bandit!"

*

Which of the following carpentry terms is most often employed discussing sex?

____ 1. Hammer
____ 2. Screw
____ 3. Nail
____ 4. Bang
____ 5. Tongue-in-groove

Which is the clearest indication that your penis is *not* the colossal show stopper you had always convinced yourself it was?

_____ 1. Girls tell you they've seen chubbier clits.
_____ 2. To give a girl six inches, you have to count the stroke on the way in *and* the way out.
_____ 3. If you want to play with yourself, you have to punch yourself in the stomach and catch the thing when it pops out.
_____ 4. Your girlfriends all call you Harvey Smallbanger.
_____ 5. You fuck Cheerios and they don't break.

*

Match the colorful expressions with what they mean in real life.

_____ 1. Carrot juice
_____ 2. Sink your dink in the pink
_____ 3. Pole vault
_____ 4. Lay some cable
_____ 5. San Quentin quail
_____ 6. Beaver dam
_____ 7. Carpet muncher
_____ 8. Head full of hammers
_____ 9. Plums

_____a. Take a shit
_____b. Dumb
_____c. Lesbian
_____d. Underage girl
_____e. Kotex
_____f. Sperm
_____g. Balls
_____h. Pussy
_____i. Fuck

*

Which of the following was the country-western song that skyrocketed Drew P. Titz to relative obscurity?

_____ 1. *Button, Button, Here Comes My Husband*
_____ 2. *All of My Dreams Are Gonna Come True, Because I'm Gonna Keep Changin' 'em 'Til They Fit What's Actually Happenin'*
_____ 3. *She'll Be Comin' Like a Fountain When She Comes*
_____ 4. *I Married A Moonshiner's Daughter, and Now She Makes Me Liquor Every Night*
_____ 5. *Deep in the Throat of Texas*
_____ 6. *She Bent Over To Look for a Needle in the Haystack and Got Pricked*
_____ 7. *In the Outhouse of Life, You Were a Splinter in My Ass*
_____ 8. *Caught in Another Crease Between the Chins of Fat City*

*

Which of the following tied for last place at *The International Best Bathroom Philosophy Competition*?

_____ 1. "If love is blind, why don't they print money in Braille?"
_____ 2. "It's not who you know, but how your wife found out you know!"
_____ 3. "Love begins when you sink in his arms, and ends with your arms in his sink!"
_____ 4. "You can't judge the pressure in the well by the length of the pump handle. Dicks, however, are a different story altogether . . ."
_____ 5. "What doth it profit a man if he gaineth the world, but lootheth hith ath?"
_____ 6. "Just because you're paranoid doesn't mean they're not out to get you!"
_____ 7. "Life is a sexually transmitted disease!"

*

Which of the following lackluster poems weren't even entered in *The Erotic Rhyme of the Year Competition, 1958* because the authors were smoking pot at a Manhattan brothel with a pride of hysterical hookers and missed the deadline?

A winded young lass named Voghill
Sat down to rest on a molehill.
The resident mole,
Stuck his nose in her hole.
Miss Voghill's O.K., but the mole's ill!

Mama's baby, Papa's maybe!

She said she was going to tea with Miss Vicki
But first she'd stop in for a bit of a quickie.
My bedroom floor's now a little bit sticky,
And Miss Vicki had tea all alone!

First I kissed her 'neath the wreath,
Then picked the hairs from 'twixt my teeth!

A sailor's daughter named Clyde
Fell into the bay at low tide.
You could tell by her squeals
That some of the eels
Were finding a safe place to hide!

*

What's the most obvious evidence that you are *really* poor??

____ 1. When the kids curse they get their mouths washed out with dust.
____ 2. You have to hock your cock.
____ 3. You can't afford to get the kids a kickball, so they have to use two turtles that are 69'ing.
____ 4. Mother has to breast-feed herself.
____ 5. You have to jerk off to feed the dog.

*

Which of the following did the nymphomaniac *really* say to the baseball team?

_____ 1. "Who's on first?"
_____ 2. "Batter up!"
_____ 3. "The catcher needs better equipment!"
_____ 4. "Hot dog here!"
_____ 5. "I have a box for the entire season!"
_____ 6. "You need bigger bats!"
_____ 7. "Use two hands!"
_____ 8. "I have last licks!"
_____ 9. "Slide!"
_____10. "Infield in!"
_____11. "I don't want any foul tips!"
_____12. "Reach for those flies!"
_____13. "Have we got any knuckle ballers?"
_____14. "Don't blame me if you go home and get thrown out!"
_____15. "The best place to go is right up the middle!"
_____16. "I'm playing the field!"
_____17. "Let's try to get a man on!"
_____18. "Who swings both ways?"
_____19. "After you're all done I'll bet my cunt will hurt!"

*

Which of the following is considered by all participants to be the grooviest nickname for anal sex?

_____ 1. Mud for my turtle
_____ 2. The old dirt road
_____ 3. Hershey's Highway
_____ 4. Skewer the manure
_____ 5. Ham slamming
_____ 6. Buttfucking
_____ 7. Cornholing
_____ 8. Tagging in the fanny
_____ 9. Greeking
_____10. Stirring lunch
_____11. Polin' the colon
_____12. Riding the baloney pony
_____13. Buggering
_____14. Ah So Ling
_____15. A helmet in the browneye
_____16. Shitting a penis
_____17. A hip full of hammer

A Few More Polish Jokes!

But, since some of us are smart asses, I have to make
them just a little tougher, gang.
So go fetch the answers across the way!

_____ 1. What happened to the Polack who put odor eaters in
his shoes?
_____ 2. How does a Polack counterfeit two-dollar bills?
_____ 3. How do you make a Polish baby buggy?
_____ 4. Why did the Polish girl douche with gunpowder?
_____ 5. How did the Polish home owner break his dick?
_____ 6. What does a Polack say before he picks his nose?
_____ 7. What was the Polish stud doing in the henhouse?
_____ 8. How do you break a Polack's finger?
_____ 9. Why did the Polish tomboy give up her career as a
bricklayer?
_____10. Why do Polacks save pop tops?
_____11. Why did the Polack put a dime in his rubber?
_____12. How did the Polack manage to kill 45 people at a
Halloween party?
_____13. How can you tell a Polish cesspool?
_____14. What does a Polish girl do after she sucks cock?
_____15. How do you take a Polish sex quiz?
_____16. Why did the Polack walk through the cow pasture?
_____17. What's the last thing they do at a Polish wedding?
_____18. How can you tell the Polack in New York City?
_____19. What do they chant at a Polish baptism?
_____20. What's the toughest Polish joke to figure out?

Answers to the brilliant setups from over yonder:

____i. So if he couldn't come, he could call!

____n. To use as class rings!

____y. Beats the shit out of me!

____g. It was stretching her snatch!

____e. Punch him in the nose!

____s. He painted his helicopter green and went as a hummingbird!

____b. It's the one with the diving board!

____h. Spits out the feathers!

____a. Just answer truesies or falsies!

____l. To fertilize his earth shoes!

____j. Erases the zeroes off of twenties!

____d. He took a dozen steps and vanished!

____m. He's the one trying to buy a prophylactic from a bag lady!

____o. Flush the punch bowl!

____k. Trying to pick up a chick!

____f. Take off its flea collar!

____p. Her box was shot!

____q. "Don't flush! Don't flush!"

____r. Trying to get a piece of the rock!

____c. Grace!

Which of the following is the all-time greatest comedian's heckler putdown line?

_____ 1. "If we wanted to hear *you*, we would have gone to *your* house!"

_____ 2. "Say it again with your teeth in?"

_____ 3. "Why don't you go home and fold fish?"

_____ 4. "Do you carry around a turkey for spare parts?"

_____ 5. "I lift my leg to your family tree!"

_____ 6. "Do you wear a corrective hat?"

_____ 7. "Are you alone tonight, or is the rest of the horse outside?"

_____ 8. "You want to laugh? Look down!"

_____ 9. "I do weddings, too, if your parents ever want to get married!"

_____10. "Save your breath! You're gonna need it to inflate your date!"

_____11. "Why don't you eat some prunes and get both ends working?"

_____12. "Go get yourself a cold water enema!"

_____13. "Get a grip on yourself! I'm sure you've rehearsed!"

_____14. "You have a lot of personality! You should have brought some of it with you!"

_____15. "Up your butt with a coconut!"

_____16. "Why don't you go pick your nose apart and see what makes it run?"

_____17. "If my ass and your face were entered in a beauty contest, the judges would scream, 'Give the prize to the one-eyed man!'"

_____18. "Why don't you go play leapfrog with a unicorn?"

_____19. "Go piss into a fan! And while you're at it, stand too close!"

_____20. "Remind me to call your parents if I ever need the blueprints to build myself an asshole!"

_____21. "I hope your next shit is square!"

_____22. "Why don't you tie a knot in your dick and go to a strip show, maybe it'll back some blood up into your brain!"

_____23. "Dust your mother for my fingerprints!"

_____24. "Did someone jerk off in your mouthwash? You sound like a dick!"

After demoralizing a heckler, a comedian will often throw an aside to the rest of the crowd. In other words, one of the following would follow any of the responses from the previous page. Which is the best?

_____ 1. "It never fails to amaze me how much damage that one extra chromosome can do!"

_____ 2. "An American Express brain, and he left home without it!"

_____ 3. "Don't pay any attention to him. His vasectomy backed up, and now his brain's tied off!"

_____ 4. "Too bad there's not as much bone in his pants as there is in his head!"

_____ 5. "This guy probably needed a tutor to pass recess!"

_____ 6. "I need this guy like the IRS needs *No Tipping* signs!"

_____ 7. "What a knucklehead! I bet his hat fits like a glove!"

_____ 8. "Too bad there's not a jockey in the house, he could ride that jackass out of here!"

_____ 9. "Hecklers are a lot like canker sores. . .
No fun, but very hard to ignore!"

_____10. "Living proof his father was bad in bed!"

_____11. "I need this guy like a mermaid needs panty hose!"

_____12. "He should rent himself out as a laxative.
He's irritating the shit out of me!"

_____13. "I'll bet if his dick were a dynamite stick, he couldn't blow his nose!"

*

Which of the following would make you notice a girl is a big, fat, fucking hog?

_____ 1. She douches with a lawn sprinkler.
_____ 2. She has to shave her legs with a chain saw.
_____ 3. Her legs are so dumpy it looks like she shit in her panty hose.
_____ 4. You give her a boot in the ass and there's room.
_____ 5. You go down on her and miss your exit.
_____ 6. She needs Velcro on her Tampax.
_____ 7. You take her to Yankee Stadium, and the game is called on account of one of her farts!
_____ 8. At the movies, not only does she take up two seats, but she can't even feel the armrest in the middle.

*

Of the swallowing, which is the funniest, most descriptive expression for a girl devouring the spermatazoa at the climax of fellatio?

_____ 1. Gulping the gravy
_____ 2. Swigging the jism
_____ 3. Laminating her larynx
_____ 4. Glugging the soup
_____ 5. Taking the charge
_____ 6. Sending the tadpoles south

*

Which of the following is the best comeback for a bald man after someone runs their hand across his bald head and says, "Feels just like my wife's ass!?"

_____ 1. "Hers is a bit smoother."
_____ 2. "That's what everybody says!"
_____ 3. "It doesn't get petted as often, though!"
_____ 4. "I don't think she shaves that close!"
_____ 5. "But it smells so much nicer!"
_____ 6. "Go fuck yourself!"

WIN A FREE ALBUM!

Send your best jokes, riddles and rhymes!
Any jokes I can use on "516-922-WINE" will win one of my
lp's or cassettes (please specify)!
For response, please send a self-addressed, stamped envelope.
For more information and a free three-color "Use Your
Finger!! 922-WINE" sticker, also send a self-addressed,
stamped envelope.
Send it all to:

Jackie "922-WINE" Martling
Box 62F
East Norwich, NY 11732

"Use Your Finger! 516-922-WINE!" has been different *every
day* for over six years, and many, many jokes have already
been on. But don't be discouraged! Give it your best shot!
If I can't use your joke(s), I'll send you a discount coupon good
towards the purchase of any of my albums!

About the Author

Jackie "922-WINE" Martling has been a professional entertainer since the age of fourteen. He started playing in a rock and roll band before the coming of the Beatles, played all through his schooling at Michigan State University (Mechanical Engineering '71), continued in a Long Island-based comedy/original music trio, the now-infamous Off Hour Rockers, and made the switch to stand-up in 1979.

Jackie has released four party albums on his own *Off Hour Rockers Records*. He can currently be seen in *Dirty, Dirty Jokes,* a videocassette hosted by Redd Foxx. *More Raunchy Riddles* is his fourth *Pinnacle* joke book.

A familiar face on comedy stages from coast to coast, Jackie's screamingly funny nightclub act makes for a memorable evening.

Rodney Dangerfield, Phyllis Diller, Rip Taylor, Jackie Mason, Howard Stern, and Pete Fogel have all used Jackie's material. Some even bought it. In early 1984 he taped two T.V. shows, one with Gabe Kaplan, and the other with Redd Foxx, but then later recorded over them.

Jackie also owns and operates "Use Your Finger! 922-WINE," the world's only x-rated joke line (516-922-9463). The laugh line, which operates around the clock, is a minute of sassy, saucy jokes, rhymes, and riddles that Jackie and his production partner Nancy Sirianni change faithfully seven days a week.

Jackie insists that his family is middle class on a good day, lives on the beautiful North Shore of Long Island, New York, and sees more biographies in his future.